HTML5 2022

THE BEST GUIDE TO FORMATTING WEBSITES AND LEARNING THE BASICS OF WEB DESIGN. USE HTML TO CREATE INNOVATIVE WEBSITES AND APPLICATIONS

INDEX

Introduction

The purpose of this guide is not only to teach you how to format in HTML5, but also to provide a critical look at programming by explaining the "behind the scenes" beyond the screen we use every day. Why?

Because everything around us is based on programming. In the era of technology, we all have to deal with this world unknown to most. We all interact with the code, not just the insiders. Our perception of the world is now strongly influenced by increasingly advanced technological tools. We use devices that contain an incredible concentration of human intelligence in a completely passive way.

Think about it.

You bought this book by placing an order online. You paid a bill through a website. In just one day, you can perform countless actions thanks to technology. Not to mention the abuse of smartphone use. According to a Lancaster University study published in the journal Plos One, we use it on average **five hours a day**, looking at it 85 times over the course of 24 hours. About a third of the time we spend awake is spent looking at the phone. The disturbing aspect is that the perception of its use is totally distorted. **People control it twice** as much as they think they do.

At this point I would say that we can write down the first good reason to learn at least the basics of programming:

1. Stop being a passive user of technology.

Some argue that programming will be a fundamental skill almost like reading and writing. In fact, code is the language of machines and machines increasingly play the role of intermediaries between us and the world. Learning this new language means gaining awareness of the mechanisms that govern the era of technology. The more aware you are, the less a slave you are to an often unjust system.

Talking like a machine allows you to "think" like a machine. Here is the second good reason:

2. Knowing how to program means knowing how to think differently.

But what exactly does it mean to program?

Programming means writing a series of instructions that will be read, interpreted and executed. Basically, programming is sustaining a conversation. The purpose of this conversation is to create something that is functional to our purpose.

To do this, it takes order.

As the legal system regulates the development of social life and the relationships between individuals, even in computer science there is a set of rules to be respected. If the rigor is lacking, the intended objective will not be achieved. A small mistake is enough to jeopardize our work. In computer science there is no place for imprecision.

3. Programming offers you the right method to unravel situations and solve problems with rigor and meticulousness.

I hope this brief introduction has helped us understand the world we are about to dive into.

I can't wait to take you on this journey!

Chapter 1. What is HTML?

What HTML is not

Let's start with what HTML **is not**. HTML is not a programming language.
How? And the whole premise about programming?
You are right but, although it is not a programming language, it remains
essential in web-oriented programming. It will therefore be the basis from
which to start, the foundation of our work.

HTML stands for **"HyperText Markup Language"**. It is, therefore, a
markup language useful for formatting documents often created to be viewed
with browsers. This is why it is good to talk about a formatting (or markup)
language rather than a programming language.
The expression "markup language" refers to a language that allows you to
describe data through specific formatting. This formatting is possible through
the aforementioned markers. In HTML we will refer to markers with the
name **tag**.

A bit of history

The HTML project was born in 1989 thanks to Tim Berners-Lee together with the HTTP protocol. The development was completed and made public in 1993 at CERN in Geneva. The world knows the first formal definition of HTML and the HTTP protocol, the two tools that have brought the Internet to every corner of the planet. In the 90s the World Wide Web spread rapidly thanks to the birth of commercial browsers. The first browser to enter homes was Netscape, followed by Microsoft's Internet Explorer which for about ten years had the hegemony of the Web.
We are talking about a public domain language which has now reached its fifth version. The syntax of HTML is established, edited and reviewed by the World Wide Web Consortium (W3C).

A bit of order

I do not want to confuse you from the first chapter with terms which, perhaps, you do not fully understand. Let's make our life easier by schematizing and reviewing the various technical terms used so far.

1. **WWW**.
   Although it is used daily, many of the people do not even know the literal meaning of the World Wide Web.
   First of all, the **Web is not the Internet**. Indeed, the Web is only one (certainly among the most important) of the many services offered by the Internet. Basically it allows us to browse and reach contents connected to each other through the famous **links**. This is

what the famous "network" we are talking about is. Obviously it would not be so intuitive to reach the aforementioned contents without a Browser and a network protocol;

2. **Internet**.

The Internet is a **telecommunications network**. What is a telecommunications network? It is the set of devices, transmission channels and procedures through which two or more users, located in different geographical positions, can exchange information. This information is transferred and received through a common network protocol suite called "TCP/IP". TCP and IP are the most important (but not the only) protocols used because they are in fact the language in which computers connected to the Internet (called "hosts") communicate with each other. It is such a widespread public access network that it connects devices all over the world. To help us, we can think of the Internet as the telephone network. Both are worldwide and publicly accessible;

3. **Client-Server Architecture.**

Indicates a network architecture in which a **client** computer connects to a server to use a certain service.

More simply, by limiting the concept to the web, we can say that **servers** are the computers that contain the physical files that make up websites, and that, through the Web, allow access to clients. What does it mean to allow access to the client?

Whenever a content or service is requested by browsing the web, a return trip is made. From a Client (e.g. computer, tablet, smartphone, etc ...) connected to the Internet, it is possible to request content from a Server which returns the requested content to the Client. But what content or services are we talking about?

Any content you see in your browser while browsing the web is returned from a call to a server: logos, images, texts, videos, etc ... It is all contained within physical files on a server. Online features and services are not excluded. For example, when you log into a private area on your home banking, all you do is make a call to your bank's server. The server will check the validity of the credentials entered and will respond to your call with the result of its check. If the credentials are correct, it will let you in, otherwise it will deny you access. This system of **request** (Client request) and **response** (Server response) is possible thanks to the Client-Server architecture. This process is feasible thanks to the set of 4 elements:

a. The **HTTP** protocol;
b. A **URL** (which also masks the Server IP Address);
c. A **Browser**;
d. And our dear **HTML**.

4. **HTTP**.

Reading up to this point, we may already have an idea of what the HTTP protocol can be. This is the set of rules and methods for transmitting information on the Web. This is why HTTP is essential in a Client-Server architecture;

5. **IP address**.

To simplify, we could say that the IP address is like the "home" address of every machine connected to the Internet. It is therefore a

unique address described (to date) with 4 numbers in decimal base (from 0 to 255) separated by the "dot" symbol.

An example of an IP address is 192.0.13.734;

6. URL.

The URL uniquely locates a computer resource. It is informally referred to as "Web Address". Normally the URL identifies web pages, photos, documents, videos and all those resources that can be recovered via the HTTP protocol, but is also used for file transfer, access to databases and much more;

7. Browser.

The Browser needs no introduction. It is probably the most used software by users. In other words, the Browser is the software (installed on the Client) that allows access to the World Wide Web (and beyond). Consequently, it allows the recovery of web resources through requests to servers and the interpretation and display of these resources. The most popular browsers are Google Chrome, Edge, Internet Explorer, Mozilla Firefox and Safari. Allow me to advise you on the use of the (alas little known) **Brave** Browser;

8. HTML.

Let's go back to the beginning. In light of what we have just said, the role of HTML should be clearer.

The main functionality of HTML is to **make the content requested by a Client accessible to a Server.** Without HTML, the Web would be usable and interpretable only by technicians and, therefore, mostly unusable by the vast majority of people.

Well, now that we have a clearer understanding of the context within which our markup language is located, we can start coding by creating our first HTML page.

Chapter 2. Writing in HTML5

To write HTML you need two tools:

    1. A Browser;

    2. A text editor;

Browser

In programming, there is no browser which is better than the others. Each browser has its own developers and, consequently, each browser will give more weight to one thing than to another.

This means that, when delivering a job, the application we develop will have to be successfully tested on all popular commercial browsers to prevent some features we have developed from not working for some users. Unfortunately or fortunately there is not a single browser: you have to deal with it.

The most popular browsers, as we have seen, are Google Chrome, Safari, Internet Explorer, Edge, Mozilla Firefox and Opera. Emerging browsers such as the aforementioned Brave should not be underestimated.

During the writing phase, we need the browser to view the HTML pages we work on and to be able to test their functionality.

Editor

The text editor is a software that allows writing. The simple Windows Notepad and Notepad and the MacOs TextEdit are sufficient to be able to write in HTML. Any program that allows composing texts will be fine for writing our first few lines of HTML. As you can imagine, however, there are some programming-specific text editors. They have the function of facilitating writing to the programmer by helping with the syntax of the language with which one is writing. Some of these editors are called **IDEs** (Integrated Development Environment). These are special editors dedicated to programming that also act as compilers and help with integration, debugging and much more.

In this guide we will use Visual Studio Code. It is a versatile and highly performing free IDE by Microsoft.

As already mentioned, to write in HTML we do not need the additional features offered by the IDE, but we will limit ourselves to using the Text Editor function. Feel free to experiment using different editors. There are many free and professional ones:

- Sublime Text;
- Atom;
- Notepad++;
- Coda;
- Brackets (simple and effective, but out of maintenance from September 2021);
- Intellij Idea;
- Komodo;
- Dreamweaver;

And many others!

To install Visual Studio Code go to the site _code.visualstudio.com_ and click the blue download button.

Once the installation is complete, open VsCode and create a new file. You can use the shortcut "command + N" on MacOs and "control + N" on Windows. Alternatively you can click "File" and "New File".

Extensions

The first thing to do, in addition to specifying the name, is to indicate the extension of our new file. Extension plays a fundamental role. If we did not write ".html" (or ".htm") the browser would not recognize the file type and would not be able to open and interpret it correctly.
Browsers, of course, also interpret other types of files and are able to read them correctly thanks to their extensions. A browser can open an image (.jpeg, .jpg, .gif, .png, .svg etc ...), an audio or video file (.mp3, .mp4, .ogg, .webm etc ...), a text (.doc), a pdf (.pdf), but it can also download a zipped file (.zip), read server-side code (.php, .asp, .jsp etc...) and much more.
In all these cases, the file extension is essential.

We then proceed naming our first HTML file. Save the file and name it "home.html" where "home" is the name and ".html" the extension.

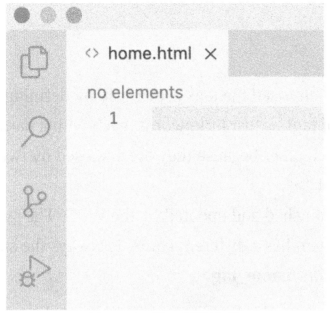

Figure 3 - First HTML file

Even the editor, for the simple fact of having added the extension to the file, has understood that we are dealing with an HTML sheet and has already prepared to help us with the syntax.

Suggestion: the file name can be alphanumeric, but the use of special characters such as!, *,., # etc ... is prohibited. Also you should always avoid using the "blank" character.
It is customary to use only **lowercase** letters to name files.

TAG

We have already mentioned the tags previously by defining them as **markers.** Think of tags as just little words, each with a particular function. They recognize each other because they are enclosed by two special characters: "<" and ">".

Tag names are established and updated by the W3C. The syntax of the tags, although each of them has a different name, is always the same: **<name_tag>***content***</name_tag>**.

Let's vivisect what we have just written:

1. **<name_tag>** - opening tag;
2. **</name_tag>** - closing tag (always has a slash before the name "/");
3. *content* – content of the tag.

Basically we are telling the browser that everything contained between the opening tag and the closing tag must be formatted according to the instructions of the tag.

Let's exemplify immediately!

To write a word or a portion of text in italics, it is necessary to enclose the aforementioned text within the opening tag ** and the closing tag **. Then *Hello World!* will appear in your browser like this: *Hello World!*

Let's try together. In the newly created file write:

```
<em>Hello World!</em>
```

Before opening the file in the browser always remember to **save**!
This is what you will see if you open the file:

Hello World!

Figure 5 - Italics (browser)

Simple, isn't it?
Note that in the search bar of the browser we have the path of the local file on our computer and not a URL of the Web. This is because we are opening with the browser a file on our computer and not loaded on a remote server (not therefore an http call is required - see chapter 1).

What happens if we remove the tag *<em>*?
The text will simply be displayed normally.

Hello World!

Figure 6 - Text without the <em> tag

At first glance it would seem that the browser is a mere pass-through and that it displays everything written in the editor without altering anything.
It is not so.

There are several things we can appreciate by looking at the words "Hello World!" in the browser. First of all, the browser chose a specific font and we certainly didn't tell it (the default font is Times New Roman). It also chose 16px as the font size in total autonomy. And, come to think of it, it also decided to write the text from left to right. It is not so obvious if you are Arab for example. Quite right?

Let's take another example. There are two tags for writing in bold: *<b>* and *<strong>*. There is no difference in the browser. What we will see in the browser with both tags will always be:

Hello World!

Figure 7 – Bold (browser)

The main difference is in **SEO** (Search Engine Optimization). I do not want to dwell on the SEO topic in this guide, but, briefly, it is a set of rules that allow you to optimize a website to improve its position in search results. Therefore, within *<strong>* it is recommended to write keywords that define well the theme of the HTML file in question (these are the famous keywords), while within *<b>* you write all those words for which you want only a graphic rendering in bold (they are not relevant).
We write in bold using the tag *<b>*:

```
<b>Hello World!</b>
```

The browser reads from top to bottom and from left to right. As soon as it encounters the "<" character, it immediately checks whether there is a tag subsequently. If so, then it will format the content of that tag according to the tag's instructions. In this case we will see "Hello World!" in bold as in Figure 7.

And ... if we wrote that?

```
< b >Hello World!</b>
```

This produces something like the following in a browser:

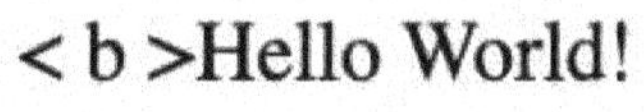

< b >Hello World!

Figure 10 - Tag error

Why?

Due to the white space left between the character "<" and the name of the tag "b", the browser no longer interprets our *<b>* as a tag, but as simple text to be printed on the page. Note that, despite being well written, the closing tag has no effect on the words "Hello World!". Unlike the opening tag, however, it is not displayed in the browser.

Before tackling chapter 3, I invite you to experiment with the use of these first HTML tags that we encountered by playing around with the various possibilities. Try making a single portion bold and not all of the text, closing a single letter within a tag, **opening a tag without closing it** or even inventing your own tag to see how the browser reacts. A fancy tag like *<hello> </hello>* is ignored or printed in the browser? find it out!

Chapter 3. Let's deepen the TAGS

In this chapter we will learn about some of the most used tags in basic HTML trying to understand even more the mechanisms behind the Web pages we are used to browsing.

Always remember that the browser does nothing (or almost nothing) unless it is first specifically asked to do so. Let's take a trivial example:

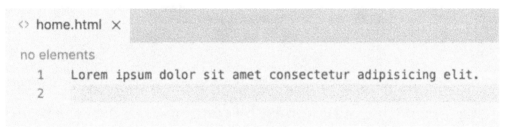

Figure 11 - Lorem ipsum

This Latin phrase is taken from the text "Lorem ipsum". It is a placeholder text used by programmers (but also graphic designers, designers and typographers) as a filler for graphic proofs.

By now you already know what you would see in the browser if you opened this file in the browser. The writing would be printed as it is.

What if you decide to wrap things up like this?

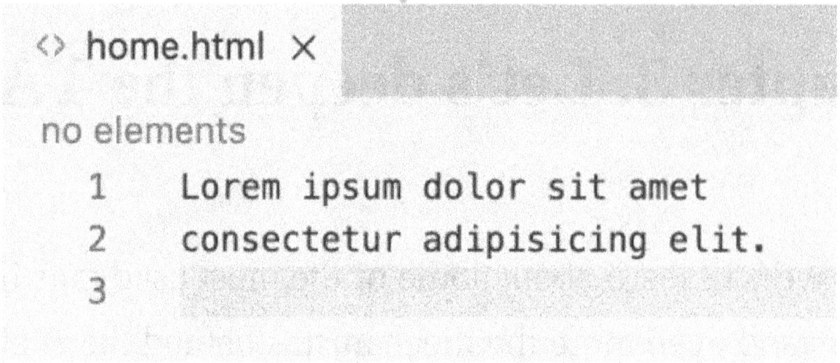

```
<> home.html  ✕

no elements
  1     Lorem ipsum dolor sit amet
  2     consectetur adipisicing elit.
  3
```

Figure 12 – Starting a new line

Let's open the browser and see what happens.

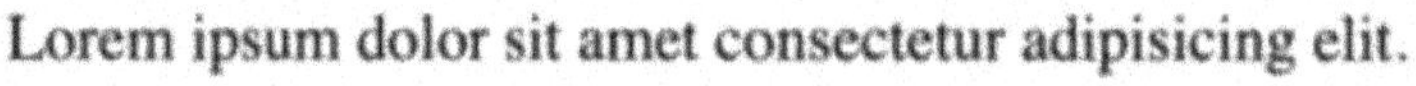

Lorem ipsum dolor sit amet consectetur adipisicing elit.

Figure 13 - The browser fails to start a new line

The browser doesn't wrap because it doesn't know it has to. Let's remember the rule: **any formatting action must be communicated to the browser**. It will not wrap unless there is a tag that tells it to do so. The specific tag for breaking is *
* (line break). The peculiarity of this tag is that it does not need a closing tag. Writing *</br>* wouldn't make any sense.
This is because the *
* tag only cares about wrapping and not formatting a piece of text. It goes without saying that, unlike the *<em>* tag for example, there will be no content in the *
* tag.

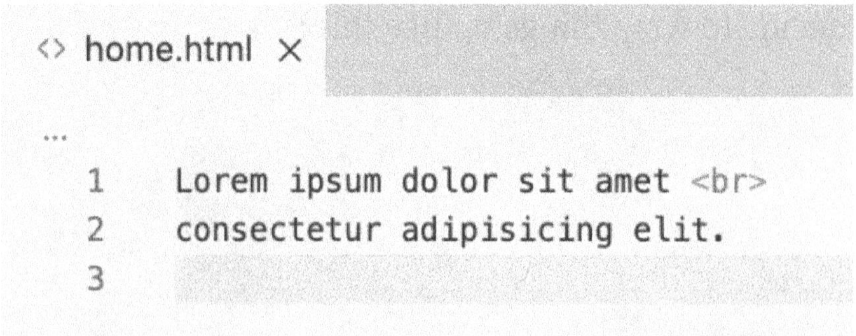

```
<> home.html  ✕

...
  1     Lorem ipsum dolor sit amet <br>
  2     consectetur adipisicing elit.
  3
```

*Figure 14 - Tag
 (editor)*

The result is the following:

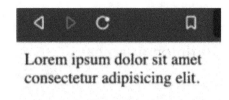

Lorem ipsum dolor sit amet
consectetur adipisicing elit.

*Figure 15 - Tag
 (browser)*

The decision to write it just after the word "amet" is completely arbitrary.

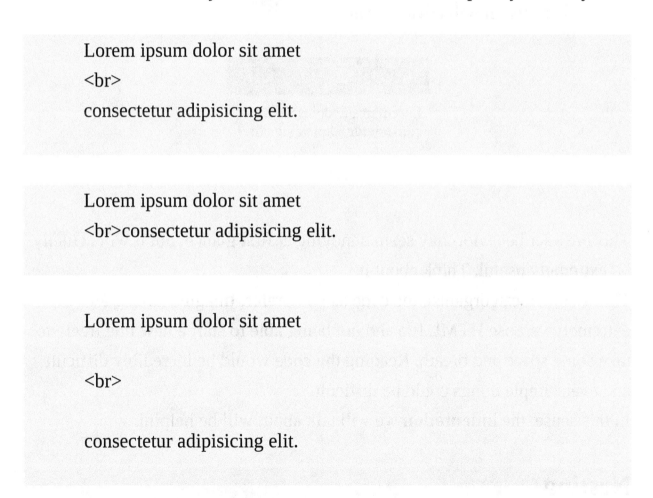

Lorem ipsum dolor sit amet

consectetur adipisicing elit.

Lorem ipsum dolor sit amet

consectetur adipisicing elit.

Lorem ipsum dolor sit amet

consectetur adipisicing elit.

Writing in these other ways would make no difference. The browser completely ignores the fact that you go to the head in the editor just as it ignores the double white space between one word and another.

Try writing like this:

Lorem ipsum   dolor sit amet

consectetur adipisicing elit.

You will see that it will always print:

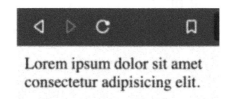

Lorem ipsum dolor sit amet
consectetur adipisicing elit.

Figure 16 - Additional whitespace is ignored

This browser behavior may seem annoying at first glance, but it will actually be extremely useful. Think about it.

This way you can organize the code as you prefer. Imagine having an extremely verbose HTML file and not being able to start a new line freely to take some space and breath. Reading the code would be incredibly difficult and even simple things could be difficult.

In this sense, the **indentation** we will talk about will be helpful.

Nesting

An important feature of HTML is that tags can be nested inside each other. In short, the content of a tag can be another tag.

<b>Lorem ipsum <br> dolor sit amet</b> consectetur adipisicing elit.

In this way the browser will turn bold from "Lorem" to "amet" making sure to start a new line after "ipsum":

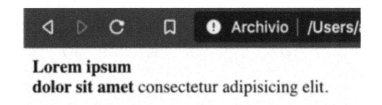

**Lorem ipsum
dolor sit amet** consectetur adipisicing elit.

Figure 17 – Nesting (browser)

Remember that tags must open and close in a **mirror image**.
A good metaphor could be that of mathematical parentheses {[(...)]}.

Let's code example using *<em>* and *<strong>*:

```
1    <em>
2        <strong>
3            Lorem ipsum <br>dolor sit amet
4        </strong>
5    </em>
6    consectetur adipisicing elit.
7
```

Figure 18 – Nesting (editor)

In Figure 18, the *<em>* tag opens before the *<strong>* tag, but closes after it.

In practice, the *<em>* tag contains the *<strong>* tag.

This type of "pyramidal" writing you see in Figure 18 is called **indentation** and is essential to increase the readability of the code.

Look at the Figure again.

One cannot avoid appreciating the clarity and readability of the code. In fact, you understand in an instant the nesting of tags, where they open and where they close. Now imagine the same code written on one line or without the pyramid structure we just saw. Although it still is a very simple code, you may have problems reading.

Try to imagine now what would happen if we did not use indentation correctly in a file of hundreds (if not thousands) of lines. It would in fact be impossible to work.

I recommend that you immediately adopt indentation even if the simplicity of the code, at the moment, leads you to think that it is not necessary. It is a "best practice" that will always come in handy.

We will have the opportunity to use it several times during this guide, so if at the moment the concept is not fully clear to you, don't worry.

Next, open the file in a browser. You will see something like this:

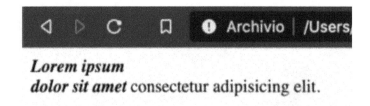

Figure 19 – Nesting tags

As you can see, the effects of tags can add up without hindering each other.

Although one is inside the other, in the browser we have the text in bold, italics and a new line after "ipsum".

The instructions can then be added and, as in arithmetic, by changing the order of the addends, in this case the tags, the result does not change.

On video we will therefore have the same result if we write as below:

```
 <> home.html  ✕

 ...
 1    <strong>
 2        <em>
 3            Lorem ipsum <br>dolor sit amet
 4        </em>
 5    </strong>
 6    consectetur adipisicing elit.
 7
```

Figure 20 - Reverse nesting

As you can imagine, if two identical tags are nested, the graphic rendering will not change.

```
<b><b>Lorem ipsum</b></b>
```

Doubling the *<b>* tag gives you the same boldface you would get with just one *<b>* tag.

<u>Pay close attention to nesting because most of the mistakes made in HTML concern the wrong closing of tags.</u>

Attributes and <a> tags

The attribute is an additional specification that can be given to a tag. Many attributes are specific to some tags; if used within different tags they would have no effect. Many others are common to different tags. We will learn about many of them throughout this guide.

The syntax is common for each attribute:

```
name_attribute="value"
```

The "=" symbol is used to divide the attribute name from its value, while the quotation marks enclose the value.

Let's exemplify by introducing a new tag: **<a>**.

The *<a>* tag is used to create links. The "a" stands for **anchor** and is not to be confused with the *<link>* tag (used to load an external resource). They're called anchors because they weren't initially designed to jump between pages (like links we're used to), but were used to link content within a specific document. As real anchors, in fact, these tags also allow you to easily move between the different sections of our html sheet (usually used in a very large sheet or on one-page websites). We will appreciate how it works in Chapter 4.

The *<a>* tag alone indicates to the browser that its content must be clickable, but an attribute is required to specify which url to reach once our link is clicked.

Therefore, it is not enough to write *<a>Click here!</a>*, but you have to add the correct attribute **inside the opening tag**. Just after the letter "a" you need to type a blank space. We can then use the *href="url"* attribute, where *href* is the type of instruction and *url* is the corresponding value.

```
<> home.html  ×

...
  1    <strong>
  2        <em>
  3            Lorem ipsum <br> dolor sit amet
  4        </em>
  5    </strong>
  6    consectetur adipisicing elit.
  7
  8    <br>
  9    <br>
 10
 11    <a href="https://www.greenpeace.org/">Click here!</a>
 12
```

Figure 21 - Link in editor

This creates the following output:

Lorem ipsum
dolor sit amet consectetur adipisicing elit.

Click here!

Figure 22 - <a> tag (browser)

Now clicking on the text portion *"Click here!"* we will be redirected to the Greenpeace homepage. As you can see, the browser, for the simple fact of encountering the *<a>* tag, colors *"Click here!"* in blue (turning it into purple after the first click), underlines it and transforms the cursor into **pointer**, that is the classic "hand", when passing over it.

Everything you write **inside the angle brackets of the opening tag** is information dedicated to the browser and **not** to users browsing the HTML page. Users, therefore, will not see the attributes, but will still benefit from their presence.

Remember that the attribute name cannot be changed, while the value can. In this case, *href* is required and immutable, while you could potentially write any *URL* as a value.

It is possible to indicate several different attributes within the same tag. For example, we could add an attribute to the *<a>* tag that tells the browser to open the link *"https://www.greenpeace.org/"* in a new tab and not in the current one. This practice is useful if you want to redirect a user to a third-party website without forcing him to leave ours.
This attribute is called *"target"* and the value needed to tell the browser to open the link in a new tab is *"_blank"*.

```
8    <br>
9    <br>
10
11   <a href="https://www.greenpeace.org/" target="_blank">Click here to open the site in another tab!</a>
12
```

Figure 23 - target attribute

Our above code would give us the following result:

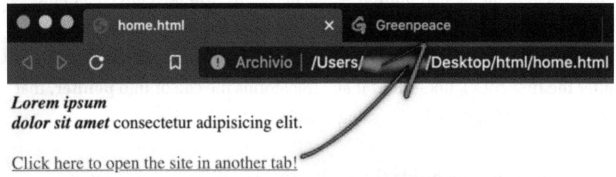

Figure 24 – Target attribute (browser)

It is completely indifferent if the position of the attributes within the tag is reversed. Writing like this would give the exact same result:

```
<a target="_blank" href="https://www.greenpeace.org/">Click here!
</a>
```

Other uses of the tag <a>

The *<a>* tag also allows us to indicate to the browser to interact with some software installed on the user's client:

1. **mailto**.
   The indication *"mailto"*, inside the *href* attribute, indicates to the browser that, upon clicking on the content of the *<a>* tag, it must open the default software dedicated to managing emails (such as the Gmail or Outlook app) and who must write in the *"to"* field the email address specified after the ":" symbol.
   In the example below, when you click on the text " *Send email!"*, The page for sending a new dedicated software email will be opened with the recipient field already filled in with *"info@test.com"*. Obviously, whatever client the user is using works. If the click is made from a smartphone, the app dedicated to email management will be opened.

   ```
   <a href="mailto:info@test.com">Send email!</a>
   ```

2. **tel**.
   The indication *"tel"* tells the browser to call the specified number. The

operation is similar to *"mailto"*. I always recommend that you also specify the prefix in case the users you are addressing are also foreigners. If the click is not made from a smartphone, the default app dedicated to calls will open, if present on the client (such as FaceTime on macos).

```
<a href="tel: +1408XXXXXXX">Call us</a>
```

3. **skype**.

The indication *"skype"* tells the browser to open the Skype software, if installed, and call the specified contact.

```
<a href="skype:john">Call John on Skype!</a>
```

Common mistakes

Don't be scared if you have problems with syntax. We are at the beginning, it is completely normal. To help you I will list some of the most common mistakes that are made when starting to write html code. This way you can focus them as points of attention and it will be easier not to repeat them. A badly written html code does not cause problems to the Browser (such as an unexpected closure of the page), but it can cause problems in the formatting of the pages; the aesthetic/functional result could be compromised.

Common mistakes:

1. If an "open" and "close" tag (for example <em>) is not closed, its effect could be very different depending on the type of browser used or the specific command. If <em> is not closed, for example, the rest of the page would be formatted in italics. It is an excellent "good practice" to **close the tag as soon as you open it** to avoid forgetting it;

2. A closing tag without the corresponding opening tag has no effect;

3. If a tag contains incorrect syntax it is almost always ignored by the browser;

4. If the conventional form of the tag is wrong, for example if the minor sign "<" is incorrectly written twice "<<", the browser will interpret it as text and show it within the web page (see also Figure 9 and 10).

Uppercase or lowercase?

HTML is **"case unsensitive"**. It means that it is completely indifferent whether the tags are written in uppercase or lowercase.
Example:

```
<a href="https://www.greenpeace.org/">Click here!</a>

<A HREF="HTTPS://WWW.GREENPEACE.ORG/">CLICK HERE!</A>
```

Both lines are read and interpreted correctly by the browser.
However, *URLs* to images and other direct references may be case sensitive. The convention is therefore to write the HTML code mainly in lowercase. As already said, however, in HTML writing in uppercase or lowercase does not constitute any error.

Chapter 4. The structure of an HTML document

Let's now see together the basic structure of an HTML document.

```
home.html  X

1   <!DOCTYPE html>
2   <html>
3       <head>
4           <meta charset="utf-8">
5           <title>Document's title</title>
6       </head>
7
8       <body>
9           It's the section of the HTML document that will be directly visible on your web page.
10      </body>
11  </html>
12
```

Figure 25 - Basic HTML document structure

Let's analyze together each element contained within Figure 25:

1. **<!DOCTYPE html>.**
   Each HTML page must start with the *doctype* declaration. This is not an HTML tag, but rather information for the browser regarding the type of document it should expect. In our case we are telling the browser that the file it is about to read is an HTML5 file. As you can imagine then, older versions of HTML have their own doctype. For example, the doctype of version 4.01 is *<! DOCTYPE HTML PUBLIC "- // W3C // DTD HTML 4.01 Transitional // EN" "http://www.w3.org/TR/html4/loose.dtd">.*

The doctype is not case sensitive. You will often find it written in lowercase and, more rarely, *<!DocType html>*;

2. **<html>**.
It is the parent tag of all the others. It represents the "root" of an HTML document by marking the beginning and end of the file;

3. **<head>**.
The *<head>* tag identifies a section in which very useful information that is not seen must be entered (with a few exceptions) by users who view the HTML document.
Within this tag we find the **metadata**. It is "data on data"; they therefore contain information relating to the HTML document in question. They are mostly defined thanks to the **<meta>** tag that we will see in point 4.
Below is a list of the most common tags used within *<head>*:
   a. **<title>** (which we will see in point 5);
   b. **<style>** - useful for embedding style sheets (CSS) within the HTML file;
   c. **<base>** - specifies the **base URL** for all relative URLs in the document (we will not use it in this guide);
   d. **<link>** - useful for loading an external resource within the document (often a style sheet);
   e. **<meta>** (see point 4);
   f. **<script>** - useful for embedding a client-side script as a piece of code in Javascript (we will not use it in this guide);

4. **<meta>**.

As already mentioned in point 3, the *<meta>* tag is responsible for defining the metadata relating to a document. They can be inserted only in the *<head>* tag and are typically used to define the set of characters that will be used in the document, to describe the page, to identify the keywords, to identify the author of the document and to set the viewport.

Line 4 in Figure 25 is essential. In each document we must always define the character set that is needed for writing. The *"charset"* attribute helps us by giving us the opportunity to specify the right value for the HTML document in question. The most used character set in the West is *"UTF-8"*. A character in UTF-8 can be 1 to 4 bytes long. This set can represent any character in the Unicode standard and is the optimal encoding for e-mails and web pages.

Have you ever noticed question marks, squares or, more generally, particular symbols within web pages? In those cases, a character that is not present in the specified charset was used in the head and therefore the browser did not know how to display it.

You may have already noticed that *<meta>* does not have a closing tag. You already know that, as in the case of *
* above, if a tag does not want content, the closing tag is not needed. Writing *</meta>* would not make sense;

5. **<title>**.

The title of the page must be inserted in the *<title>* tag. It is one of the few pieces of information in the *<head>* tag that is visible to users. By reloading the file you should be able to see the title in the browser tab.

The title is essential for several reasons. In addition to being useful to users if there are many opened tabs in the browser, it is one of the most important factors for SEO purposes (mentioned in chapter 2). The title, in fact, is also **the title that appears in the SERPs of search engines**. (SERPs are Search Engine Results Page).

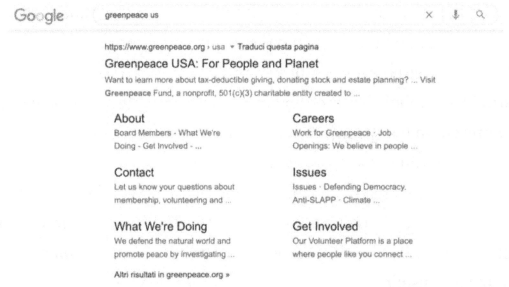

All the texts you see in blue in the figure above are the titles of the individual HTML pages. Always remember to enter it!

Also remember that HTML does not think with us, it just does what we write. Nothing prevents you, in fact, from giving the same title to multiple pages, but it is quite logical that doing so would be wrong. Always give the title based on the content of your HTML document;

6. **\<body\>**.

With the *\<body\>* tag we close our basic structure. As you may have already guessed, the content of the *\<body\>* tag is basically everything the user sees on the browser. In fact, it contains all the contents of an HTML file: navigation menus, paragraphs, multimedia contents, links, tables, lists, compilation forms, footers, etc ...

All the examples we have done in the previous chapters will always be placed in the *\<body\>* tag.

Let's put what we have learned into practice by creating a newspaper article together. You will see that with a little practice you will digest these concepts well and it will be easier and easier for you to "tinker" with HTML!

Let's create a newspaper article

Let's open a new HTML file and name it *"article.html"*.
The first thing to do is to rebuild the basic HTML structure:

```
<> article.html  ✕

...
1    <!DOCTYPE html>
2    <html>
3        <head>
4            <meta charset="utf-8">
5            <title></title>
6        </head>
7
8        <body>
9
10       </body>
11   </html>
12
```

Figure 26 – Base structure for our article

Now let's give our document a title.

```
<head>
        <meta charset="utf-8">
        <title>My article</title>
</head>
```

Always check that every time you make a change to the HTML file
everything is fine in your browser. This way you can check the correctness of
your actions from time to time.

Now let's write some placeholder text in the *<body>* to compose our article always using "Lorem ipsum".

```
8    <body>
9        Lorem Ipsum
10
11       by John Doe
12
13       Lorem ipsum dolor sit amet consectetur adipisicing elit. Laudantium maxime quibusdam fugiat molestias veniam
         accusamus necessitatibus nulla quos nemo consectetur, distinctio ipsum eligendi!
14
15       Index
16
17       Ut enim
18       Duis aute
19       Excepteur sint
20
21       Ut enim
22
23       Lorem ipsum dolor sit amet consectetur adipisicing elit. Cumque soluta temporibus assumenda beatae sapiente
         ipsam sequi praesentium repellendus. Vitae aut, et dolores ex iste fugiat quam porro fugit nulla! Ducimus.
24       Lorem ipsum dolor sit amet consectetur, adipisicing elit. Optio, nihil quis quaerat officia perspiciatis quasi
         explicabo natus minima doloremque eum, nisi repellendus modi, sit laboriosam provident corporis facere
         exercitationem blanditiis!
25
26       Duis aute
27
28       Lorem ipsum dolor sit amet consectetur adipisicing elit. Eos, architecto dolore in quae recusandae assumenda
         soluta fugit at optio qui illum voluptatum ex? Nam repellat porro optio dolorem possimus expedita. Lorem ipsum
         dolor sit amet consectetur adipisicing elit. Quisquam tempora saepe maxime cupiditate minima asperiores
         laboriosam dolore accusantium commodi optio, ipsam doloribus velit, neque nostrum, fugit sapiente iste
         voluptatem hic.
29
30       Excepteur sint
31
32       Lorem ipsum dolor sit amet consectetur adipisicing elit. Facere maxime nisi obcaecati reiciendis. Iste nostrum
         dolore nihil doloremque beatae recusandae sint eius ipsum, omnis facilis fugiat fugit quae tempora velit.
         Lorem ipsum dolor sit amet consectetur adipisicing elit. Obcaecati tenetur fugiat doloribus molestiae dolorem
         eos vitae officia debitis. Itaque sit suscipit hic fuga quia, dolores beatae quod doloremque earum similique.
33
34   </body>
```

Figure 28 – Article body

Let's format it this way:

- Line 9 -> Main heading;
- Line 11 -> Author name;
- Line 13 -> Introduction paragraph;
- Line 15 -> Subheading for the index;
- From line 17 to line 19 -> Index;
- Line 21 -> Subheading;
- Line 23 -> Paragraph;
- Line 26 -> Subheading;

- Line 28 -> Paragraph;
- Line 30 -> Subheading;
- Line 32 -> Paragraph.

You already know what we would see if we saved the file as it is and opened it with the browser, right?

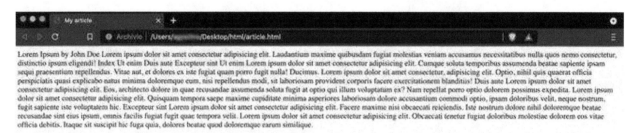

Figure 29 - Unformatted article

Always remember that manually wrapping without tags in the editor has no effect in the browser.

First, let's format the main title of our article on line 9.

Titles

There is a specific tag to format the titles and it consists of the letter "h" and a number from 1 to 6. The number establishes the importance and size of the title.

```
<h1>Heading 1</h1>
<h2>Heading 2</h2>
<h3>Heading 3</h3>
<h4>Heading 4</h4>
<h5>Heading 5</h5>
<h6>Heading 6</h6>
```

<h1> is the most important title and it is a good rule to use one per page as it represents the main header/subject of the entire document. It is another good habit **not to skip header levels**: start with *<h1>*, then use *<h2>*, and so on. We use the *<h1>* tag on line 9.

```
<body>
    <h1>Lorem ipsum</h1>
```

Figure 30 - Tag <h1>

Let's save and reload the browser tab.

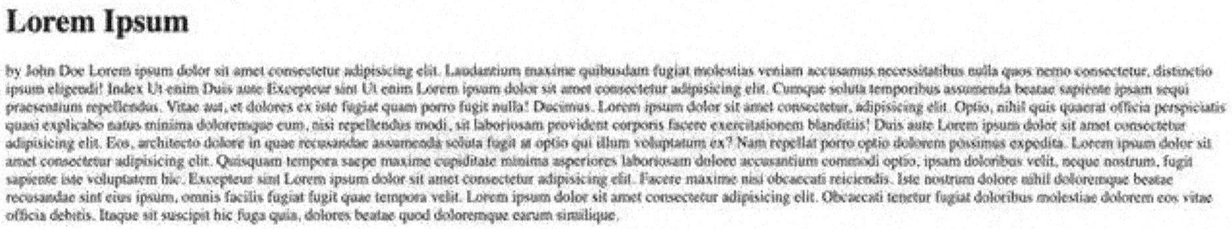

Lorem Ipsum

by John Doe Lorem ipsum dolor sit amet consectetur adipisicing elit. Laudantium maxime quibusdam fugiat molestias veniam accusamus necessitatibus nulla quos nemo consectetur, distinctio ipsum eligendi! Index Ut enim Duis aute Excepteur sint Ut enim Lorem ipsum dolor sit amet consectetur adipisicing elit. Cumque soluta temporibus assumenda beatae sapiente ipsam sequi praesentium repellendus. Vitae aut, et dolores ex iste fugiat quam porro fugit nulla! Decimus. Lorem ipsum dolor sit amet consectetur, adipisicing elit. Optio, nihil quis quaerat officia perspiciatis quasi explicabo natus minima doloremque eum, nisi repellendus modi, sit laboriosam provident corporis facere exercitationem blanditiis! Duis aute Lorem ipsum dolor sit amet consectetur adipisicing elit. Eos, architecto dolore in quae recusandae assumenda soluta fugit at optio qui illum voluptatum ex? Nam repellat porro optio dolorem possimus expedita. Lorem ipsum dolor sit amet consectetur adipisicing elit. Quisquam tempora saepe maxime cupiditate minima asperiores laboriosam dolore accusantium commodi optio, ipsam doloribus velit, neque nostrum, fugit sapiente iste voluptatem hic. Excepteur sint Lorem ipsum dolor sit amet consectetur adipisicing elit. Facere maxime nisi obcaecati reiciendis. Iste nostrum dolore nihil doloremque beatae recusandae sint eius ipsum, omnis facilis fugiat fugit quae tempora velit. Lorem ipsum dolor sit amet consectetur adipisicing elit. Obcaecati tenetur fugiat doloribus molestiae dolorem eos vitae officia debitis. Itaque sit suscipit hic fuga quia, dolores beatae quod doloremque earum similique.

Figure 31 - Tag <h1>(browser)

The *<h1>* doubled the size of the text from 16px to 32px, made it bold, created a space above and below called **margin** and started a new line (note that we did not use any *
).*

We use the *<em>* tag to make the author name italic in line 11 and add two *
* tags to start a new line twice, leaving a space line between the author name and the rest of the article.

```
<body>
    <h1>Lorem Ipsum</h1>

    <em>by John Doe</em>
    <br>
    <br>
    Lorem ipsum dolor sit amet consectetur adipisicing elit. Laudantium maxime quibusdam fugiat molestias veniam
    accusamus necessitatibus nulla quos nemo consectetur, distinctio ipsum eligendi!
```

Figure 32 - Tag <em> for the author's name

Let's reload the tab.

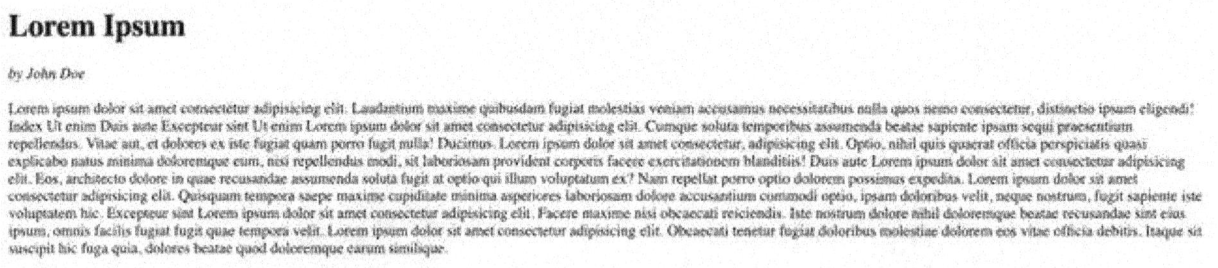

Figure 33 - Author name in italics

Although the graphic result is exactly what we were looking for, in this case it is more appropriate to use the tag dedicated to paragraphs *<p>*.

Paragraphs

As anticipated, the **<p>** tag identifies a paragraph. When the browser encounters this tag, it automatically adds a blank line above and below the portion of text contained between the opening tag and the closing tag. Let's try using it in our example on line 13 to format our introduction paragraph. Remember to delete the previously added *
* tags because, as already mentioned, the *<p>* tag already has a margin by default that separates the text block from the rest (a bit like the titles from *<h1>* to *<h6>*).

```
<body>
    <h1>Lorem Ipsum</h1>

    <em>by John Doe</em>
    <p>
    Lorem ipsum dolor sit amet consectetur adipisicing elit. Laudantium maxime quibusdam fugiat molestias veniam
    accusamus necessitatibus nulla quos nemo consectetur, distinctio ipsum eligendi!
    </p>
```

Figure 34 - Tag <p> (editor)

Let's check the browser.

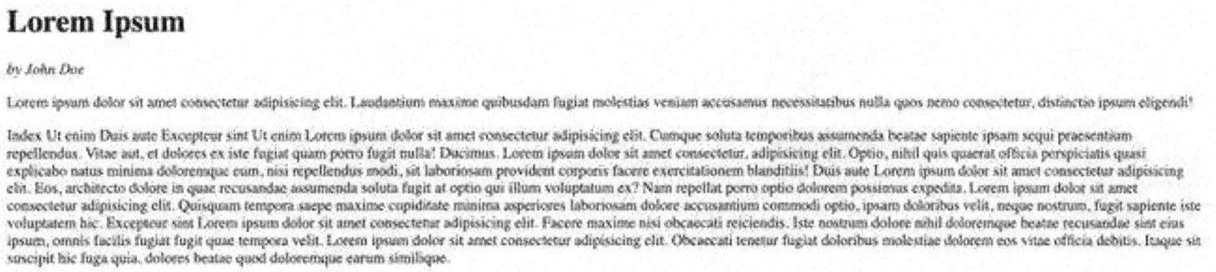

Lorem Ipsum

by John Doe

Lorem ipsum dolor sit amet consectetur adipisicing elit. Laudantium maxime quibusdam fugiat molestias veniam accusamus necessitatibus nulla quos nemo consectetur, distinctio ipsum eligendi!

Index Ut enim Duis aute Excepteur sint Ut enim Lorem ipsum dolor sit amet consectetur adipisicing elit. Cumque soluta temporibus assumenda beatae sapiente ipsam sequi praesentium repellendus. Vitae aut, et dolores ex iste fugiat quam porro fugit nulla! Ducimus. Lorem ipsum dolor sit amet consectetur, adipisicing elit. Optio, nihil quis quaerat officia perspiciatis quasi explicabo natus minima doloremque eum, nisi repellendus modi, sit laboriosam provident corporis facere exercitationem blanditiis! Duis aute Lorem ipsum dolor sit amet consectetur adipisicing elit. Eos, architecto dolore in quae recusandae assumenda soluta fugit at optio qui illum voluptatum ex? Nam repellat porro optio dolorem possimus expedita. Lorem ipsum dolor sit amet consectetur adipisicing elit. Quisquam tempora saepe maxime cupiditate minima asperiores laboriosam dolore accusantium commodi optio, ipsam doloribus velit, neque nostrum, fugit sapiente iste voluptatem hic. Excepteur sint Lorem ipsum dolor sit amet consectetur adipisicing elit. Facere maxime nisi obcaecati reiciendis. Iste nostrum dolore nihil doloremque beatae recusandae sint eius ipsum, omnis facilis fugiat fugit quae tempora velit. Lorem ipsum dolor sit amet consectetur adipisicing elit. Obcaecati tenetur fugiat doloribus molestiae dolorem eos vitae officia debitis. Itaque sit suscipit hic fuga quia, dolores beatae quod doloremque earum similique.

Figure 35 – Tag <p> (browser)

Let's get on with the work and format the text blocks on lines 23, 27 and 31 as paragraphs.

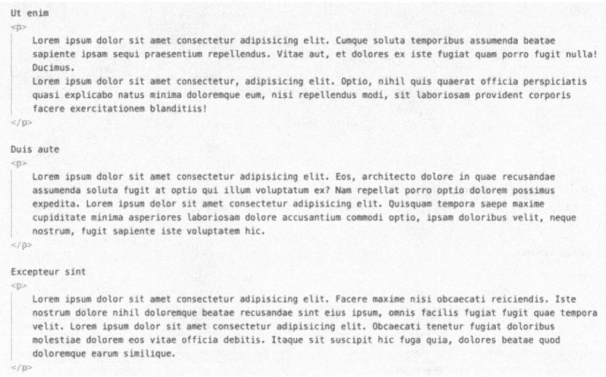

```
Ut enim
<p>
    Lorem ipsum dolor sit amet consectetur adipisicing elit. Cumque soluta temporibus assumenda beatae
    sapiente ipsam sequi praesentium repellendus. Vitae aut, et dolores ex iste fugiat quam porro fugit nulla!
    Ducimus.
    Lorem ipsum dolor sit amet consectetur, adipisicing elit. Optio, nihil quis quaerat officia perspiciatis
    quasi explicabo natus minima doloremque eum, nisi repellendus modi, sit laboriosam provident corporis
    facere exercitationem blanditiis!
</p>

Duis aute
<p>
    Lorem ipsum dolor sit amet consectetur adipisicing elit. Eos, architecto dolore in quae recusandae
    assumenda soluta fugit at optio qui illum voluptatum ex? Nam repellat porro optio dolorem possimus
    expedita. Lorem ipsum dolor sit amet consectetur adipisicing elit. Quisquam tempora saepe maxime
    cupiditate minima asperiores laboriosam dolore accusantium commodi optio, ipsam doloribus velit, neque
    nostrum, fugit sapiente iste voluptatem hic.
</p>

Excepteur sint
<p>
    Lorem ipsum dolor sit amet consectetur adipisicing elit. Facere maxime nisi obcaecati reiciendis. Iste
    nostrum dolore nihil doloremque beatae recusandae sint eius ipsum, omnis facilis fugiat fugit quae tempora
    velit. Lorem ipsum dolor sit amet consectetur adipisicing elit. Obcaecati tenetur fugiat doloribus
    molestiae dolorem eos vitae officia debitis. Itaque sit suscipit hic fuga quia, dolores beatae quod
    doloremque earum similique.
</p>
```

Figure 36 - Let's format the other paragraphs

We check the browser again to make sure that the formatting is identical to the introduction paragraph.

Lorem Ipsum

by John Doe

Lorem ipsum dolor sit amet consectetur adipisicing elit. Laudantium maxime quibusdam fugiat molestias veniam accusamus necessitatibus nulla quos nemo consectetur, distinctio ipsum eligendi!

Index Ut enim Duis aute Excepteur sint Ut enim

Lorem ipsum dolor sit amet consectetur adipisicing elit. Cumque soluta temporibus assumenda beatae sapiente ipsam sequi praesentium repellendus. Vitae aut, et dolores ex iste fugiat quam porro fugit nulla! Ducimus. Lorem ipsum dolor sit amet consectetur, adipisicing elit. Optio, nihil quis quaerat officia perspiciatis quasi explicabo natus minima doloremque eum, nisi repellendus modi, sit laboriosam provident corporis facere exercitationem blanditiis!

Duis aute

Lorem ipsum dolor sit amet consectetur adipisicing elit. Eos, architecto dolore in quae recusandae assumenda soluta fugit at optio qui illum voluptatum ex? Nam repellat porro optio dolorem possimus expedita. Lorem ipsum dolor sit amet consectetur adipisicing elit. Quisquam tempora saepe maxime cupiditate minima asperiores laboriosam dolore accusantium commodi optio, ipsam doloribus velit, neque nostrum, fugit sapiente iste voluptatem hic.

Excepteur sint

Lorem ipsum dolor sit amet consectetur adipisicing elit. Facere maxime nisi obcaecati reiciendis. Iste nostrum dolore nihil doloremque beatae recusandae sint eius ipsum, omnis facilis fugiat fugit quae tempora velit. Lorem ipsum dolor sit amet consectetur adipisicing elit. Obcaecati tenetur fugiat doloribus molestiae dolorem eos vitae officia debitis. Itaque sit suscipit hic fuga quia, dolores beatae quod doloremque earum similique.

Figure 37 – Paragraphs (browser)

Great, it works. Let's proceed with the subtitles for the index and for the individual paragraphs. We know which tags to use, right?

```
<h2>Index</h2>
```

Figure 38 - <h2> tag for the index

```
<h3>Ut enim</h3>
<p>
    Lorem ipsum dolor sit amet consectetur adipisicing elit. Cumque soluta temporibus assumenda beatae
    sapiente ipsam sequi praesentium repellendus. Vitae aut, et dolores ex iste fugiat quam porro fugit nulla!
    Ducimus.
    Lorem ipsum dolor sit amet consectetur, adipisicing elit. Optio, nihil quis quaerat officia perspiciatis
    quasi explicabo natus minima doloremque eum, nisi repellendus modi, sit laboriosam provident corporis
    facere exercitationem blanditiis!
</p>

<h3>Duis aute</h3>
<p>
    Lorem ipsum dolor sit amet consectetur adipisicing elit. Eos, architecto dolore in quae recusandae
    assumenda soluta fugit at optio qui illum voluptatum ex? Nam repellat porro optio dolorem possimus
    expedita. Lorem ipsum dolor sit amet consectetur adipisicing elit. Quisquam tempora saepe maxime
    cupiditate minima asperiores laboriosam dolore accusantium commodi optio, ipsam doloribus velit, neque
    nostrum, fugit sapiente iste voluptatem hic.
</p>

<h3>Excepteur sint</h3>
<p>
    Lorem ipsum dolor sit amet consectetur adipisicing elit. Facere maxime nisi obcaecati reiciendis. Iste
    nostrum dolore nihil doloremque beatae recusandae sint eius ipsum, omnis facilis fugiat fugit quae tempora
    velit. Lorem ipsum dolor sit amet consectetur adipisicing elit. Obcaecati tenetur fugiat doloribus
    molestiae dolorem eos vitae officia debitis. Itaque sit suscipit hic fuga quia, dolores beatae quod
    doloremque earum similique.
</p>
</body>
```

Figure 39 - <h3> tag for paragraph subtitles

The resulting UI looks something like this:

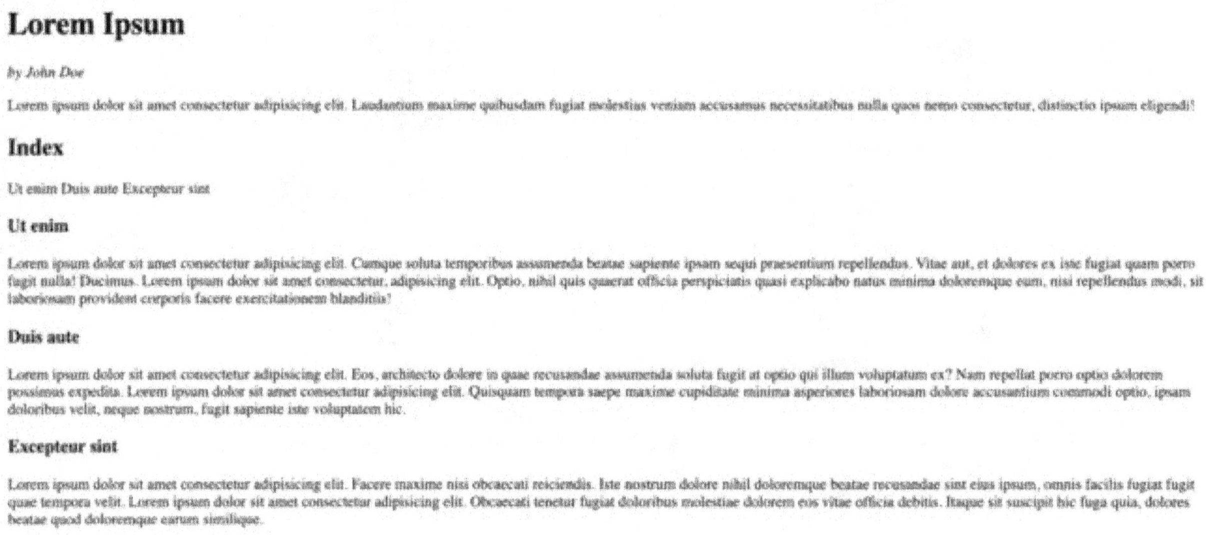

Lorem ipsum dolor sit amet consectetur adipisicing elit. Laudantium maxime quibusdam fugiat molestias veniam accusamus necessitatibus nulla quos nemo consectetur, distinctio ipsum eligendi!

Index

Ut enim Duis aute Excepteur sint

Ut enim

Lorem ipsum dolor sit amet consectetur adipisicing elit. Cumque soluta temporibus assumenda beatae sapiente ipsam sequi praesentium repellendus. Vitae aut, et dolores ex iste fugiat quam porro fugit nulla! Ducimus. Lorem ipsum dolor sit amet consectetur, adipisicing elit. Optio, nihil quis quaerat officia perspiciatis quasi explicabo natus minima doloremque eum, nisi repellendus modi, sit laboriosam provident corporis facere exercitationem blanditiis?

Duis aute

Lorem ipsum dolor sit amet consectetur adipisicing elit. Eos, architecto dolore in quae recusandae assumenda soluta fugit at optio qui illum voluptatum ex? Nam repellat porro optio dolorem possimus expedita. Lorem ipsum dolor sit amet consectetur adipisicing elit. Quisquam tempora saepe maxime cupiditate minima asperiores laboriosam dolore accusantium commodi optio, ipsam doloribus velit, neque nostrum, fugit sapiente iste voluptatem hic.

Excepteur sint

Lorem ipsum dolor sit amet consectetur adipisicing elit. Facere maxime nisi obcaecati reiciendis. Iste nostrum dolore nihil doloremque beatae recusandae sint eius ipsum, omnis facilis fugiat fugit quae tempora velit. Lorem ipsum dolor sit amet consectetur adipisicing elit. Obcaecati tenetur fugiat doloribus molestiae dolorem eos vitae officia debitis. Itaque sit suscipit hic fuga quia, dolores beatae quod doloremque earum similique.

Figure 40 - Subheadings (browser)

Well, we just have to format the index as a **list**.

Lists

There are two tags for formatting a list: **<ul>** (unordered list) and **<ol>** (ordered list).

As the names suggest, the former is for formatting unordered lists (so-called bulleted lists), while the latter formats ordered lists (numbered lists).

It is not enough, however, to write in the following way:

```
<ul>
    Guitar
    Bass
    Drums
</ul>


<ol>
    Violin
```

```
        Viola
        Cello
    </ol>
```

In the browser, in fact, the *<ul>* and *<ol>* tags only deal with indenting the list and detaching it from the rest of the text with a little margin. The individual items, therefore, are not stacked one on top of the other, but are shown side by side. We therefore need a specific tag that formats the components of the list one by one. Maybe you are thinking of using the tag *
* and intuition is not bad. Using the *
*, however, would not create a new entry in the list, but would simply wrap in the first entry. Try thinking about lists in Word software. Whenever you press the "Enter" key you create a new bulleted or numbered entry, but you could also press "Shift + Enter" if you wanted to. In that case, you would wrap staying in the current entry and not creating a new one.

Unlike *
*, the *<li>* (list item) tag is perfect.

Let's try to use them all to format our index. Duplicate the text and put it inside the *<ul>* and *<ol>* tags, as we did for musical instruments just before. Now every single item must be contained within *<li></ li>*.

```
<h2>Index</h2>

<ul>
    <li>Ut enim</li>
    <li>Duis aute</li>
    <li>Excepteur sint</li>
</ul>

<ol>
    <li>Ut enim</li>
    <li>Duis aute</li>
    <li>Excepteur sint</li>
</ol>
```

Figure 41 - Lists in editor

Your finished lists should look something like the following:

Index

- Ut enim
- Duis aute
- Excepteur sint

1. Ut enim
2. Duis aute
3. Excepteur sint

Figure 42 - Lists (browser)

Always remember that *<li>* must always be included within *<ul>* or *<ol>*. Using it independently would not make sense.

Don't worry about the look and feel of our HTML document. Think of

HTML as the skeleton of our page; it is not its job to improve the aesthetics and usability of a website.

A solid and well-written HTML code will be the ideal basis for aesthetically transforming the page with style sheets (CSS).

The list is an HTML structure in which you can clearly see the potential of the nesting we talked about in chapter 3. You can potentially nest indefinitely by inserting other tags inside *<li>*. You can nicely think of tags as matryoshkas. Try writing the *<b>* tag inside one of the *<li>* tags that we have in the code to make that single item bold. Then add to same item the *<em>* tag for italics and the *<a>* tag to transform it into a link. You will see that there are no limits.

I am writing it with you to give you a reference (pay attention to my use of indentation).

```
<ul>
    <li>
        <b>
            <em>
                <a href="https://en.wikipedia.org/wiki/Matryoshka_doll">
                    Ut enim
                </a>
            </em>
        </b>
    </li>
    <li>Duis aute</li>
    <li>Excepteur sint</li>
</ul>
```

Figure 43 - Nesting

Now the entry "Ut enim" is in bold, in italics and is also a link that leads to the Wikipedia page of the matryoshka.

What if we wanted to create a sub-list of the second item "Duis aute"?
All we have to do is nest again by opening another *<ul>* or *<ol>* within the
<li> tag in question.

```
        </b>
    </li>
    <li>Duis aute
        <ol>
            <li>Test 1</li>
            <li>Test 2</li>
            <li>Test 3</li>
        </ol>
    </li>
    <li>Excepteur sint</li>
```

Figure 44 - Nested list

Please note that the new list *<ol>* has been opened between the end of the
content of the *<li>* tag we have chosen (so immediately after the word
"aute") and its closing tag *</li>*. You can easily nest *<ol>* lists within *<ul>*
lists and vice versa.

Now reload the file in your browser. You should see something like this:

- ***Ut enim***
- Duis aute
    1. Test 1
    2. Test 2
    3. Test 3
- Excepteur sint

1. Ut enim
2. Duis aute
3. Excepteur sint

Figure 45 -Nested list

The "Matryoshka" logic never fails in HTML. You can also here, potentially indefinitely, nest other sublists in the just nested new list.

You may be wondering what all this stuff has to do with websites. On the other hand, what is the use of nesting a list?

Just to give you an example, today the list is the classic HTML structure used to create navigation menus and the sub-lists are often the drop-down menus that usually open when the cursor moves over the menu items.

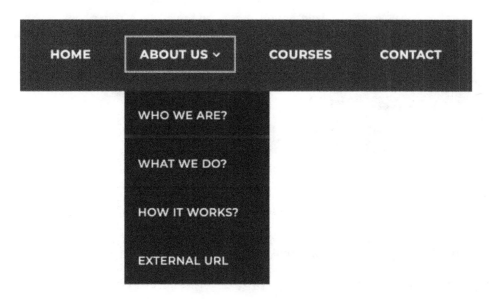

Figure 46 - Navigation menu with <ul> and <li> with CSS

The HTML behind the menu you see in Figure 46 is nothing more than a *<ol>* list with a sub-list nested in the *<li>* tag of the "About us" item. There is no difference with the HTML we wrote to format the list and sub-list in Figure 44. Remember that HTML is the skeleton and structure of a website. The CSS language is concerned with "styling" an HTML document. It basically decides how the HTML elements are to be displayed. The same HTML skeleton, therefore, can be displayed in different ways and forms based on the CSS we decide to apply it.

It is likely that behind every "grouping" of items or information you notice while surfing the web there is a list.

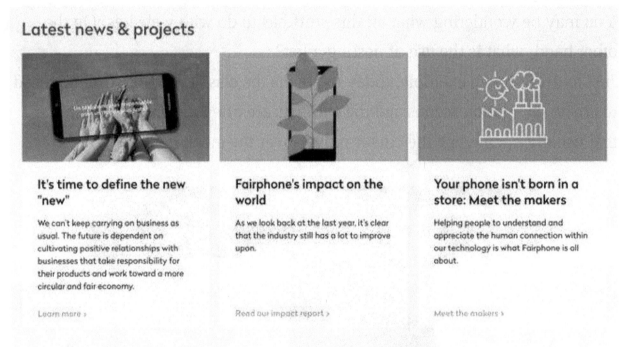

Latest news & projects

It's time to define the new "new"

We can't keep carrying on business as usual. The future is dependent on cultivating positive relationships with businesses that take responsibility for their products and work toward a more circular and fair economy.

Learn more ›

Fairphone's impact on the world

As we look back at the last year, it's clear that the industry still has a lot to improve upon.

Read our impact report ›

Your phone isn't born in a store: Meet the makers

Helping people to understand and appreciate the human connection within our technology is what Fairphone is all about.

Meet the makers ›

Figure 47 - Lists usage on the web

For example, these three article previews are structured thanks to three *<li>* tags contained within a parent *<ul>* tag.
You will see that a solid knowledge of HTML will allow you to easily create modern, intuitive, aesthetically pleasing and user-friendly web pages.

Let's proceed with the construction of our newspaper article by inserting a link at the end of the page that allows the user to obtain more information on the subject. We learned how to insert links in Chapter 3.
We insert our *<a>* tag after the closing tag of the last paragraph and write the url of the website dedicated to the text "Lorem ipsum" in the *href* attribute.
We take the opportunity to also use the target attribute with the value *"_blank"* to open the link in a new browser tab.

```
       doloremque earum similique.
   </p>

   <a href="https://www.lipsum.com/" target="_blank">Tell me more</a> about Lorem Ipsum.

</body>
```
Figure 48 - Link at the end of the article

Anchors

Now let's slightly fill in the three paragraphs with some text and some *
* tags in order to vertically lengthen the browser tab and bring out the vertical scroll bar of the browser. In this way we can take advantage of the **anchor** function of the *<a>* tag we talked about in chapter 3.

This function allows us to link elements within the same HTML document. The first thing to do is to make our three paragraphs **identifiable**. To do this we will use the *"id"* attribute. Basically, this attribute allows us to give a unique reference to any HTML tag. Let's use it inside the opening tag of each individual subtitle *<h3>* that introduces our paragraphs. As a unique value we write the first word of the subtitle.

```
<h3 id="ut">Ut enim</h3>
<p>
```
Figure 49 - Id attribute for the first subtitle

```
<h3 id="duis">Duis aute</h3>
<p>
```
Figure 50 - Id attribute for the second subtitle

```
<h3 id="excepteur">Excepteur sint</h3>
<p>
```

Figure 51 - Id attribute for the third subtitle

What we want to do is reach these elements by clicking on the relevant items in the numbered index *(<ol>)*.

To do this, we write the *<a>* tag nested in the three *<li>* of the list and value the *href* with the syntax *#name_id*.

```
<ol>
    <li><a href="#ut">Ut enim</a></li>
    <li><a href="#duis">Duis aute</a></li>
    <li><a href="#excepteur">Excepteur sint</a></li>
</ol>
```

Figure 52 - href with id

The expected behavior in the browser is the reaching of our anchors by clicking on the items in the index. Try clicking on the "Duis aute" item. The browser will behave like this.

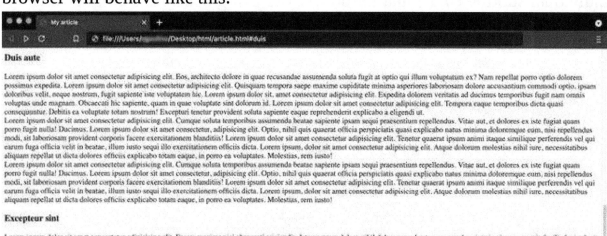

Figure 53 - Anchors in the browser

It will move you to the HTML element with the id attribute equal to that present in the *href* of the clicked *<a>* tag. The reached HTML element will always be the first to be displayed on the page. In fact, you can see how, in Figure 53, the subtitle "Duis aute" is displayed at the top of the page. Also note the path present in the browser search bar. At the click, the id of the HTML tag we have reached is added at the end.

Now try to go back to the index and click the other two items. The effect will be the same.

To conclude the article, have fun inserting some *<b>*, *<strong>* and *<em>* tags in order to format it even more.

Responsive web design

Note the "elasticity" of our HTML document. Try decreasing the size of the window browser. You will notice that the texts constantly adapt to the current window size and the annoying horizontal scroll bar does not appear.

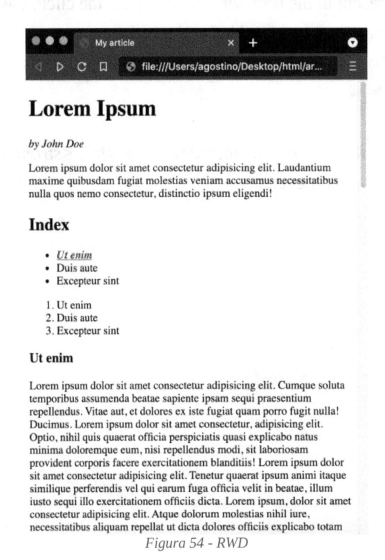

Figura 54 - RWD

This is a not indifferent feature. It basically means that if you opened this HTML file from your smartphone you would see the contents of the page perfectly suited to the size of the device you are using. It is a fundamental concept when it comes to responsive web design (**RWD**). It is a web design technique for the creation of sites capable of automatically adapting graphically to the different resolutions of the devices (think of different computers, tablets, smartphones, mobile phones, smart TVs, etc.), minimizing the need for users to resize and scroll contents. Responsive design is one of the priorities when writing CSS.

Chapter 5. Absolute and relative paths

Whenever you need to click on a word or, more generally, a content to redirect the user to another resource (a web page, multimedia content, downloadable content, etc.) or, even, to show an image in the browser, or, again, to load an external resource useful for the functionality of our HTML page (a specific font to use, a style sheet, etc.) it is mandatory to specify a **path**. Websites are in fact organized into folders and subfolders just like we organize the documents on our computer every day. The paths are used to be able to move between the folders on our website.

We have already seen some of them when we set the *href* attribute in the *<a>* tag. We have in fact specified the url of the web page that interested us at that time (see Figures 21 and 43).

In that case we used an **absolute path**.

Absolute path

The absolute path is a valid indication regardless of where it is given. Let's imagine we want to reach the Colosseum in Rome. The absolute path in this case is the address of the monument: *Piazza del Colosseo, 1, 00184 Roma RM*.

It makes no difference if we are in one point or another, if we are in north Rome or south Rome, if we are in Bologna or Bari, in Krakow or in San José: with this address we will always be able to reach the Colosseum.

To summarize, we can say that the absolute path is independent from where it is called.

Here is an example of an absolute path: *https://static.gibson.com/product-images/Custom/CUSVXV696/Bourbon_Burst/front-300_600.png*.

It is an image of a guitar.

Let's analyze the components of this path:

1. **https://** - Instructs the browser to surf the web with the https protocol. If we removed it, the browser would look for the image inside our root. We will understand this better when we see the relative paths;

2. **static.gibson.com** – Refers to the *static.gibson.com* website (it is in fact the main folder of the site);

3. **product-images/Custom/CUSVXV696/Bourbon_Burst** – Indicates that the resource (the image of the guitar) is inside a folder called *Bourbon_Burst*, which is contained within the *CUSVXV696* folder, contained within the *Custom folder*, contained inside the *product-*

images folder;

4. **front-300_600.png** – Identifies the image thanks to the name and extension *.png*.

The function of the slash character "/" should be emphasized. Every time the browser encounters the slash it understands that it must "go inside" the specified folder. *Bourbon_Burst/front-300_600.png* instructs the browser to enter the *Bourbon_Burst* folder and search inside for the *front-300_600.png* resource. The browser distinguishes a folder from a resource because the first does not have an extension.

So why is this path absolute? Because we can follow it whatever our starting point is (even from our simple *article.html* file). Obviously, the absolute path, as well as the relative path, will lose effectiveness if the resource is moved. If the Gibson website administrator decides to move that image to another folder or simply rename it, our absolute path will no longer be valid and will need to be replaced (otherwise we will see an error in the browser). It is a bit like if they were moving the Colosseum (difficult to think). In that case, the address *Piazza del Colosseo, 1, 00184, Rome, RM* will no longer be valid.

Relative path

Let's go back to the previous example. Let's imagine we want to reach the Colosseum in Rome without using the absolute path.

The relative path is an indication **depending** on where we are. For example, if we are in Piazza Venezia in front of the Altare della Patria, the relative path will be "take Via dei Fori Imperiali and continue straight to the Colosseum". As you can easily deduce, this indication does not apply if the starting point changes. If the starting point is Piazza del Popolo, Via dei Fori Imperiali will not be found (because it is not there) and the Colosseum will not be reached. This is exactly what happens when the browser does not find a resource and displays an error page: in that case the path we followed is wrong.

The relative path is related to the web page from which it is called.

Figure 55 – Relative paths

In Figure 55 you can see the directory (folder) of a website named *www.mywebsite.com*. The relative path to follow to go from the *index.html file* to *news2.html* is *Documents / News / news2.html*.

Why?

Because *news2.html* is located inside the News folder which is itself contained in Documents. Since *index.html* is at the same level as the Documents folder, we can write *Documents/* to tell the browser to enter the *Documents and News/* folder to make it enter the *News* folder. Once there we can safely access the *news2.html* file.

So if we wrote *<a href="Documenti/News/news2.html">Open news2</a>* inside the *index.html* file we would create a link that would allow us to open the *news2.html* file.

Let's code.

Open with vscode the folder in which you created the two *article.html* and *home.html* files in order to view it on the left of the editor in the "Explorer" section. From here click the button to create a new file (circled in red in Figure 56).

Figure 56 - Create a new file via editor

Let's name it *index.html* and write the basic HTML structure.

Now let's create a subfolder with the button adjacent to the one in Figure 56 and name it *documents*. Inside we create a file named *document.html* and write the usual structure.

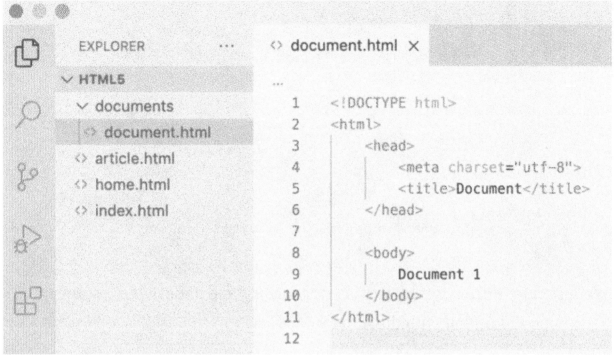

Figure 57 – document.html

In the body of *document.html* I simply wrote "Document 1". Now what we want to do is open document.html with one click starting from *index.html*. As we saw with the example in Figure 55, we just need to write a link with the correct relative path within *index.html*.

```
    <> index.html  ×    <> document.html

 1    <!DOCTYPE html>
 2    <html>
 3        <head>
 4            <meta charset="utf-8">
 5            <title>Index</title>
 6        </head>
 7
 8        <body>
 9            <h1>Relative paths</h1>
10            <a href="documents/document.html">Click here to open the document</a>
11        </body>
12    </html>
13
```

Figure 58 - Link between HTML files with relative path

We just enter *documents* by writing *documents/* and choose the resource. Now open *index.html* with the browser.

Relative paths

Click here to open the document

Figure 59 - index.html

When the link is clicked, the browser will open the correct file.

Document 1

Figure 60 - document.html

Take a look at the search bar in Figure 60. What you see is the absolute path of the *document.html* file. Here we can appreciate the usefulness of the relative path. If we have to connect two resources that are already inside the html folder, it makes no sense to also write */Users/username/Desktop/html/* because we are already inside the same root.

Relative paths are much more used than absolute paths because within the root (main folder of the website) it is always recommended to prefer relative paths. Whenever you need to reach a resource in your root from a file in your root use relative paths. Why?

Because you will often have to refer to documents located on your own website (imagine having to link the homepage to the *About Us* page via the navigation menu), so each file already shares the same starting point (www.yoursite.com). Imagine the root of your site as your home. If you have to reach a room starting from inside the house you will certainly not use an absolute path, right? You will of course use a relative path based on your current location. It doesn't make much sense, so start, repeating, for each path, *http://www.yoursite.com/* because you are already inside your site.

Also, in the development stage of the website, you have no way to work with absolute paths to link internal documents because your site is not yet on a web server. However, if you decide to work with absolute paths, you will necessarily have to change them all when publishing the site (the loss of time and the margin of error would be very high).

Finally, relative path-based code can be replicated or moved easily without having to change the links (as long as the folder structure is maintained).

We now insert a link in *document.html* to return to *index.html*.
We could use the absolute path by writing:

```
<a href="/Users/username/Desktop/html/index.html">Back to
Index</a>
```

But, as we have learned, the path could be simplified by making it relative.
Instead of going into a folder, this time you need to exit *documents* to
encounter the *index.html* file.
To tell the browser to leave a folder just write 2 dots and 1 slash: "**../**".

```
<body>
    Document 1
    <a href="../">Back to index</a>
                    <> article.html
                    🗀 documents/
                    <> home.html
                    <> index.html
```

Figure 61 – Use of "../"

As you can see, as soon as we write "../" the editor suggests the resources that
can be reached at this "level", that is, in the main working folder. This means
that if you type "../" a second time you could go back to the folder that
includes your working subfolder and so on until you reach the highest level.
In short, thanks to the use of "/" and "../" you can easily move between
folders and connect all the resources you want.
We conclude our example by selecting *index.html* and enclosing the word
"Document 1" in a tag *<h1>*.

```
<body>
    <h1>Document 1</h1>
    <a href="../index.html">Back to index</a>
```

Figura 62 - <h1> e relative path

Reload the page in your browser and check the link is working correctly.

Document 1

Back to index

Figure 63 – Relative path with "../"

If the syntax is correct, the browser will open *index.html* when clicked.

Images and paths

Let's test the paths again by introducing the *"<img>"* tag dedicated to inserting images in an HTML document.

The *<img>* tag, like the *<a>* tag, does not work if you do not specify the path to the image you want to show. To do this, we need to add the *"src"*:

```
<img src="path_image ">
```

There is no closing tag *</img>* as there is no content.

Let's go to *pixabay.com* to download a copyright-free image and save it in our workbook. You can of course use any of your other images for this test. In our *index.html* file we write the *<img>* tag specifying the relative path of our newly downloaded image. Before doing this, let's draw a dividing line to separate us from the title and link previously written with the *<hr>* tag. This tag is typically used as a content separator and is interpreted by the browser as a horizontal line.

```
<body>
    <h1>Relative paths</h1>
    <a href="documents/document.html">Click here to open the document</a>

    <hr>

</body>
```

Figure 64 - Tag <hr>

Now let's move on to the image.

```
<img src="html-image.jpeg">
```

Remember, this relative path is valid because the image is at the same level as the *index.html* file. Reload the browser tab.

Figure 66 - Image in the browser

The image is displayed correctly, but, as you can easily see, its dimensions are so large that it even shows the vertical and horizontal scroll bar.
To work around this problem, the **width** and **height** attributes can be used. The first is used to set the width of an element, the second for the height. Different units of measurement can be used for both values (em, rem, percentage values, points, etc.). The measurement unit used by default is the pixel (px).

We add the width attribute and value it with "400".

N.B. Writing width="400" is equivalent to writing width ="400**px**".

```
<img src="html-image.jpeg" width="400">
```

Here's the output:

Relative paths

Click here to open the document

Figure 68 - Shrunken image

By making it smaller, the image is certainly more usable. As you can see, changing the width of an element also changes the height in order to preserve the original size. If we wanted to specify a different value for the *height* instead, we should use the height attribute. We set 400 pixels here too in order to make the image square.

<img src="html-image.jpeg" width="400" height="400">

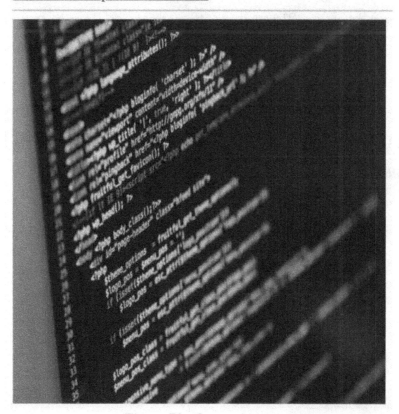

Figure 70 - Square image

You can set any value according to the needs of the moment. We can also decide to go crazy and set 1000 as *width* and 1 as *height*. In this case the image would be so fine as to appear as a line.

N.B. Shrinking or enlarging an image with attributes or style sheets **does not mean reducing its weight**. It is a good rule, in fact, to cut the image file to the maximum size you need (with the help of editing software such as Photoshop and other similar ones). There is no point in uploading a 5000px-sized photo and then having to resize it later in HTML. Why?
Because the lighter the images are, the less space the server will require for their storage and, last but not least, the images affect the heaviness of each single page of the site and the loading speed. **Always make sure you have light and fast web pages**. Pages with these characteristics are very popular with search engines and will help you improve their position in the SERPs.

I recommend that you immediately organize your workbook into neat subfolders. Create a folder dedicated to images so that you can group all the ones you will need there. Move the image to the newly created folder and reload the page.

Relative paths

Click here to open the document

Figure 71 – Image not found

The image is no longer shown because the browser cannot find it. The path in the *src* attribute of the *<img>* tag, in fact, has not been updated after the image file has been moved to the newly created *images* folder. The icon of the image cut in two appears whenever the browser follows the wrong path. Before correcting it, however, I want to advise you on the use of a new attribute. This is **alt** and is used to specify alternative text in the event that the image is not loaded (just like in figure 71). It serves to make the web page more user-friendly by giving the user a description of the image that he should have been able to see. More importantly, alt text is used by **screen-readers**, that is, by those special browsers used by blind or visually impaired people. It is also very useful for SEO because it allows you to provide search engines (or better, their spiders) with all the information they need.

```
<img src="html-image.jpeg" width="400" alt="HTML code">
```

Let's reload the page.

Relative paths

Click here to open the document

HTML code

Figure 73 - Alternative text in the browser

The text that appears is exactly what we specified in Figure 72. Now let's correct the relative path by entering the *images* folder we created.

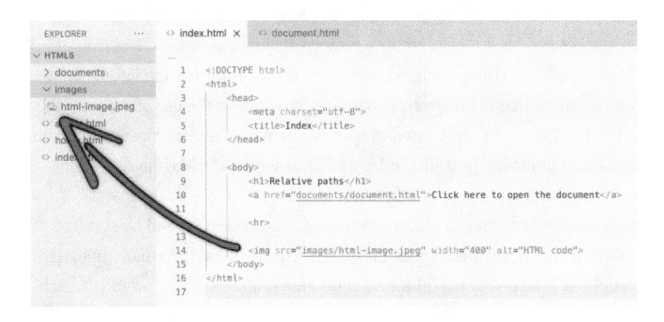

Figure 74 - Relative path correction

Reload the page and make sure the browser displays the image.

What if we wanted to view the image in *documents.html*?

It's easy! We just need to write the *<img>* tag specifying the correct path. In this case we should exit the documents folder with "../" and enter the *images* folder:

<img src="../images/html-image.jpeg" width="400" alt= "HTML Code">

Obviously, we can also insert an absolute path in the *src* attribute. It is usually done when we need to view an image that does not belong to our website or to which we do not own the rights. In Figure 75 I wrote a new *<img>* tag and enhanced the *src* attribute with the web address of the same image that we previously downloaded and saved in the *images* folder.

I separated the two images with two *<h3>* subtitles and decreased the width from 400 to 200 pixels. I take this opportunity to also show you the use of *title*. This is an additional attribute of the *<img>* tag not to be confused with *alt*. It is used to give further information about the image you are viewing and appears in the browser as a tooltip when you pause move the cursor over the image. It can be used on any HTML element (not just images).

```
<h3>Relative</h3>
<img src="../images/html-image.jpeg" width="200" alt="HTML Code" title="HTML Code">

<h3>Absolute</h3>
<img src="https://cdn.pixabay.com/photo/2016/11/18/14/80/code-1839406_960_720.jpg" width="200" alt="HTML Code"
title="HTML Code">
</body>
```

Figure 75 - Absolute path and title attribute

In the browser you will have the same image twice: one uploaded from the *images* folder on our computer, the other from the Pixabay server.

The "HTML code" label you see is the tooltip generated by the title attribute.

Document 1

Back to index

Relative

Absolute

Figure 76 - Tooltip title

The most used image formats on the web are .jpg, .jpeg, .gif and .png.

Chapter 6. Form

The forms allow the user to interact with the website he is browsing. Whenever you subscribe to a platform, log in, fill out a contact form or a form to send information you are using a ***<form>*** tag. In reality, the examples of use of a form are numerous and the possibilities they grant are just as many. This is why learning how to build a form is essential; if you want to become a web designer or a web developer you must absolutely be familiar with this tag.

Think of a contact form: basically the form is used to collect user data (name, surname, telephone, message, etc ...) to use them later. It is immediately clear that there are two well-defined moments, or phases: **filling** in the form in the browser and **processing** the data entered.

For the first you need an HTML page that shows in the browser the form fields you need, for the second you need a page with server-side code that collects, processes and saves the data. In this guide we will deal with the first phase, as the second requires knowledge of languages such as php, jsp, aspx or others.

The <form> tag

The *<form>* tag is the container for the individual fillable fields. It is a block element (remember the display property seen in chapter 6) that contains all the elements with which the user can interact.

This tag has three basic attributes: "***name***", "***action***" and "***method***".

```
        <form name="form-name" action="server.php" method="post">
</form>
```

1. ***name***.

   This attribute allows you to give the form a name. This is an optional field, but I recommend that you adopt the good habit of always writing it down. It will come in handy if you are using Javascript. Conceptually it is similar to the *id* attribute, but it serves different purposes. It must be unique and, in the case of the *<form>* tag, is used as a reference when the data is sent. It can be used on other tags such as *<iframe>* and *<meta>* and on form field tags such as *<input>*, *<button>*, *<textarea>* and *<select>* which we will see shortly;

2. ***action***.

   The action attribute can only be used in the *<form>* tag and resembles the now familiar *href*. In fact, it indicates **where to send the data** of a form when **submitting** (sending).

   Taking the example above, when the user clicks the button dedicated to sending data, the latter are directed to the *server.php* page where they will be processed. Obviously the *server* name and the *.php* extension are completely arbitrary. In general, in the *action* attribute you must specify the page you created, with server-side code (also called back-end), dedicated to processing the form data;

3. ***method***.

    In the method attribute we can specify the data "shipping" method, ie **how** to send the collected data. There are two usable values: *get* and *post*.

    a. **get**.

        It is the default value and sends the data by appending them to the URL in **name** and **value** pairs.

        Let's exemplify.

        Let's say you have a simple form with two fields: name and surname. We populate these fields with "Bob" and "Dylan" respectively. Upon clicking the submit button, you will be redirected to the page specified in the action attribute (we still use *server.php*) adding, after the *.php* extension, the names of the fields followed by an equal and the value entered by the user: "*www.mysite.com/server.php?name=Bob&surname=Dylan*". Note that the name/value pairs are separated from the extension by a *question mark* and are separated from each other by an *ampersand*. We will do the same code example shortly so you can understand better.

        Remember that the length limit of a URL is around 3000 characters. Always keep this in mind when building a form.

        Be careful not to set the get method on a form that manages sensitive data because they will be visible and, therefore, easily attacked;

b. **post**.

Submit form data with a **http transaction**. The http "transaction" consists of a connection to the server, a request from the client, a response from the server (which can send the requested data or refuse to deliver that information) and a closure. Basically, the post method affixes the form data inside the body of an http request. The data is therefore not visible in the URL as in the case of the *get* method. Furthermore, there are no limits on the size of the request and it is the suitable method for sending sensitive data. We will make a practical example immediately after having seen the other tags that make up an HTML form.

The \<input\> tag

\<input\> identifies most of the fillable fields through which the user can enter data. It can be viewed in many ways by the browser based on the value of the *type* attribute.

Below is a list of all attributable values in alphabetical order:

```
<input type="button">
<input type="checkbox">
<input type="color">
<input type="date">
<input type="datetime-local">
<input type="email">
<input type="file">
<input type="hidden">
<input type="image">
<input type="month">
<input type="number">
<input type="password">
<input type="radio">
<input type="range">
<input type="reset">
<input type="search">
<input type="submit">
<input type="tel">
<input type="text">
<input type="time">
<input type="url">
```

```
<input type="week">
```

Let's see some of them in a new *form.html* file.

Text

```
<body>
    <input type="text">
</body>
```
Figure 101 – Text input (editor)

Here's the output in the browser.

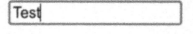
Figure 102 - Text input (browser)

This is the most common input and allows you to write any character inside it. I recommend that you always use the **<label>** tag together with *<input type="text">*, *<input type="checkbox">*, *<input type="radio">*, *<input type="file">* and *<input type="password">*. This tag is responsible for affixing a label to the input in order to specify the type of information that the user must enter inside. Visually it is no different from plain text, but it can be manipulated with CSS. So why should it be used? A first good reason is related to browser screen-readers that will read the content for people with vision problems when the user acquires focus on the field (the focus is when the cursor is in the field as in Figure 102). Furthermore, some users may have problems clicking on very small inputs (think of checkboxes for example). The label comes in handy because clicking on it will activate the corresponding input. To connect a label to its input, the value of its "*for*" attribute must be equal to the value of the input *id* attribute (Figure 103). Another way to connect the two elements is to nest the input inside the label (Figure 104).

```
<body>
    <label for="name">Name</label>
    <input type="text" id="name">
</body>
```

Figure 103 – For attribute

```
<body>
    <label>Name
        <input type="text">
    </label>
</body>
```

Figure 104 - Iinput/label nesting

Name [   ]

Figure 105 - Input text with label (browser)

Checkbox

The checkbox is displayed as a small tickable square.

They are used to allow the user to select one or more options from a limited number of choices.

```
<h2>Checkbox</h2>
<h4>Pick Your Favorite Star Wars Characters:</h4>

<input type="checkbox" id="character1" name="character1" value="Anakin">
<label for="character1"> Anakin</label>
<br>
<input type="checkbox" id="character2" name="character2" value="Obiwan">
<label for="character2"> Obiwan</label>
<br>
<input type="checkbox" id="character3" name="character3" value="Leia">
<label for="character3"> Leia</label>
<br>
<input type="checkbox" id="character4" name="character4" value="Yoda">
<label for="character4"> Yoda</label>
```

Figure 106 - Input checkbox

The finished example should look similar to the following page. Notice that you have the opportunity to check and uncheck.

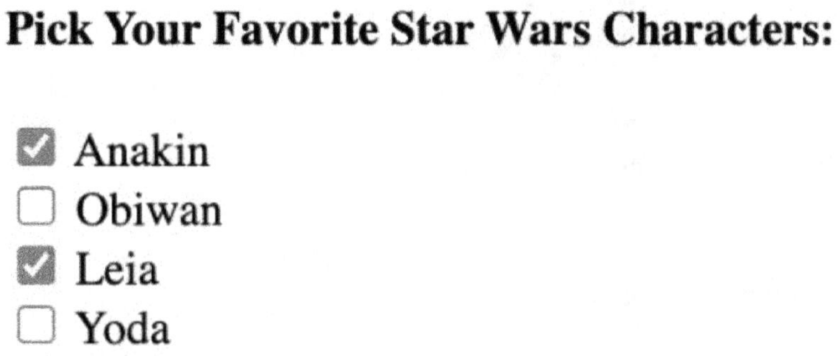

Pick Your Favorite Star Wars Characters:

- ☑ Anakin
- ☐ Obiwan
- ☑ Leia
- ☐ Yoda

Figure 107 - Checkbox (browser)

Also and above all in this case, the *<label>* tag is essential to make users understand what the checkbox list options are. The value of the *"value"* attribute, on the other hand, is not shown in the browser, but represents the value that is sent to the back-end associated with the name (*name* attribute) of the input. In the example in Figure 107, the data will be sent in the form of a name / value pair: **character1=Anakin** and **character3=Leia**. If the *value* attribute is omitted, the default value becomes **on** (*character1=on*).

Radio

The radio is usually displayed with a selectable circle. It is always found in a group, never alone. This is because the radio, unlike the checkbox, allows the user to select only one option from the available choices. Not surprisingly, in Figure 108, all radios share the same value of the *name* attribute. It is essential to consider radios as part of a group because only in this way it will be possible to make the choice of an option exclusive. In fact, once the group is created, as soon as a radio is selected, the previously selected one is automatically deselected.

```
<h2>Radio</h2>
<h4>Which Star Wars character is your favorite?</h4>

<input type="radio" id="character5" name="starWarsCharacter" value="Anakin">
<label for="character5">Anakin</label>
<br>
<input type="radio" id="character6" name="starWarsCharacter" value="Obiwan">
<label for="character6">Obiwan</label>
<br>
<input type="radio" id="character7" name="starWarsCharacter" value="Leia">
<label for="character7">Leia</label>
<br>
<input type="radio" id="character8" name="starWarsCharacter" value="Yoda">
<label for="character8">Yoda</label>
```

Figure 108 – Radio input

Also in this case the label is fundamental. Open your browser and try to select radios. Make sure that the automatic deselection mechanism works and that only one radio can be selected at a time. If it doesn't work, check the values of the *name* attributes of your radios and make sure they are the same.

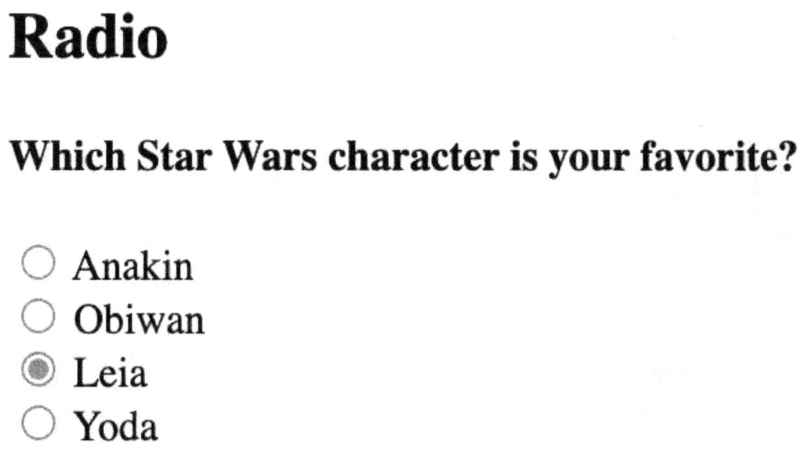

Radio

Which Star Wars character is your favorite?

- ○ Anakin
- ○ Obiwan
- ◉ Leia
- ○ Yoda

Figure 109 – Radio input (browser)

Here, too, the data is sent in the form of a name / value pair (***starWarsCharacter=Leia***) and, if the *value* attribute is omitted, the default value becomes *on*.

Button, Submit and Reset

A **button** input is displayed by the browser as a simple key. It has no default functionality; in fact it is used to activate, usually with Javascript, a function built ad hoc. Basically, it is defined in another language which behavior must occur when the button is clicked.

Here the value of the *value* attribute takes the form of a label.

```
<input type="button" value="Click Me">
```

Figure 110 – Button type input

Figure 111 - Button input (browser)

If you don't specify any value, you will see an empty button in the browser.

The **submit** type is displayed exactly like the button type, but takes care of sending all the values of the form filled in by the user to the so-called "*form-handler*". The *form-handler* is nothing more than the server-side page that is specified in the action attribute of the *<form>* tag. It goes without saying that, if you need to send data to the back-end, the submit type is essential.

The **reset** type also looks like a very common button, but, unlike its cousins button and submit, it resets the fields of the form.
Although *<input type="button">* is absolutely valid and supported by every browser, today there is a tendency to use a new specific tag for keys called *<button>*. What we have said so far about button input also applies to *<button>*.

Let's build our first form using two text inputs and the three buttons we encountered. In the example we want to allow the user to be able to send his name and surname to the back-end.
Let's open the *<form>* tag and write the three fundamental attributes seen above. We value *name* with *myForm*, *action* with *server.php* and *method* with *get*. Inside we write two text type inputs with the corresponding label. Remember to value the name attribute in the two inputs in order to distinguish the two fields.
We then add a submit button to send the data to *server.php*, reset to empty the

fields and button. Obviously, the latter will have no effect because it needs a function in another language.

I take advantage of this example to introduce a couple of interesting attributes. "**Placeholder**" serves to give a brief suggestion to the user on the type of value that is expected in a field. This indicative value is shown in gray within the input before the user writes anything.

"**Required**" enables native browser validation that prevents data from being sent if the field with the *required* attribute has not been filled in.

```html
<form name="myForm" action="server.php" method="get">

    <label>Name
        <input type="text" name="name" placeholder="Name" required>
    </label>
    <br>
    <br>
    <label>Last Name
        <input type="text" name="lastname" placeholder="Last Name" required>
    </label>
    <br>
    <br>
    <input type="submit" value="Send data">
    <input type="reset" value="Reset">
    <input type="button" value="Click Me">
</form>
```

Figure 112 - Form with input text, submit, reset and button

Let's reload the page.

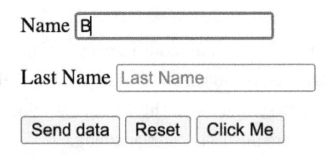

Figure 113 – Form with placeholder

Notice how the *Name* field *placeholder* disappears the moment you start typing something. To test the *required* attribute, however, just click the submit input without filling in both fields.

Figure 114 - Attribute validation required

This browser validation will not appear when the other two buttons are clicked because it is only useful when sending data (only submit action). Let's try to fill in both fields and click submit again.

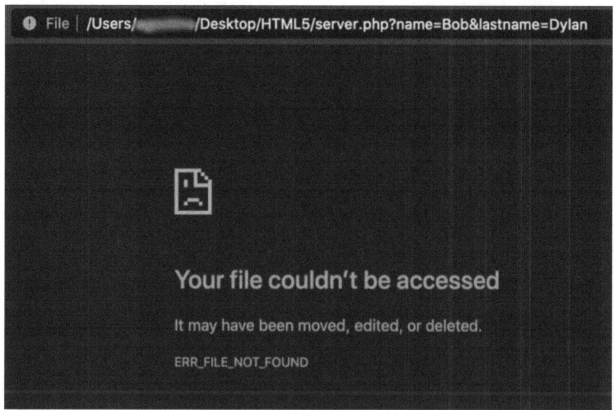

Figure 115 – Sending data to server.php

As expected, you are redirected to *server.php*. Not only. As we mentioned previously, the data, with the get method, are placed in a name/value pair in the URL. The portion of a URL that contains data to be passed as input to a page, in this case, on the server side is called **query string** (*name=Bob&lastname=Dylan*).

Obviously the browser shows us an error page because the *server.php* resource does not exist in the *html* folder. The php language is certainly not the subject of this guide, but, to avoid getting the error message, let's try to create the *server.php* page and write a simple message that the data has been received.

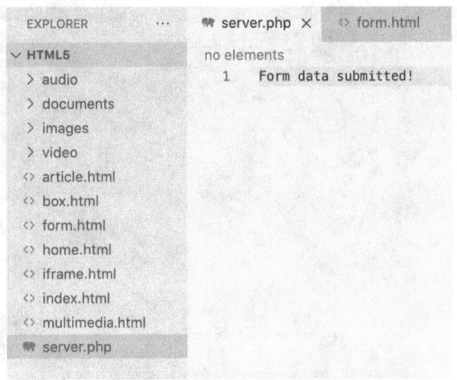

Figure 116 - Server.php page

We fill out the form again and click the send data button.

Figure 117 - Server.php page (browser)

The browser is now able to find the resource correctly.

Let's change the submission form method from get to post. We reload the page and send the data again.

Figure 118 – Post method

As you can see, the data is now not affixed to the end of the URL, but is sent by populating the body of the request. To view it you can open the browser's "developer tools". In Google Chrome or Brave, open the browser menu in the upper right corner of the window and select "More tools" and "Developer tools". You can also use the shortcut Option + ⌘ + J (on macOS), or Shift + CTRL + J (on Windows/Linux). The menu of each browser is unique although many are similar. If you do not find the button and the shortcut does not work you can try to right click on the page and select "Inspect".

Once opened, click on the "Network" tab, reload the *form.html* page and send the data again.

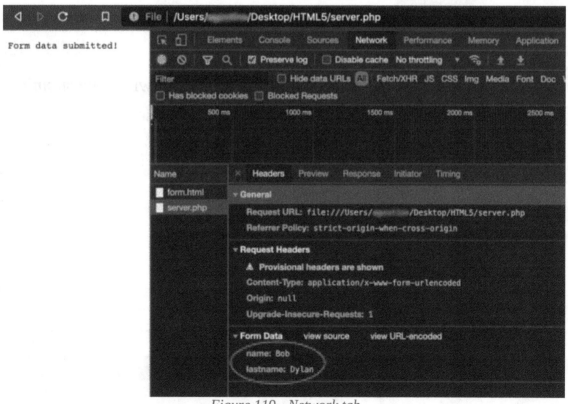

Figure 119 - Network tab

Among the uploaded resources you should find the *server.php* file to which the name/value pairs of the form have been sent.

Now test the other two buttons. At the click of the *reset* button the fields will be cleared, while at the click of the *Click Me* button there is no expected behavior.

Email

The *email* type was introduced with HTML5 and allows native client-side validation of the browser.

```
<label>Email
    <input type="email" name="email" placeholder="Email" required>
</label>
```

Figure 120 – Email type

The browser controls are triggered by the click of input with type *submit*. First, the browser makes sure that the at sign "@" is present.

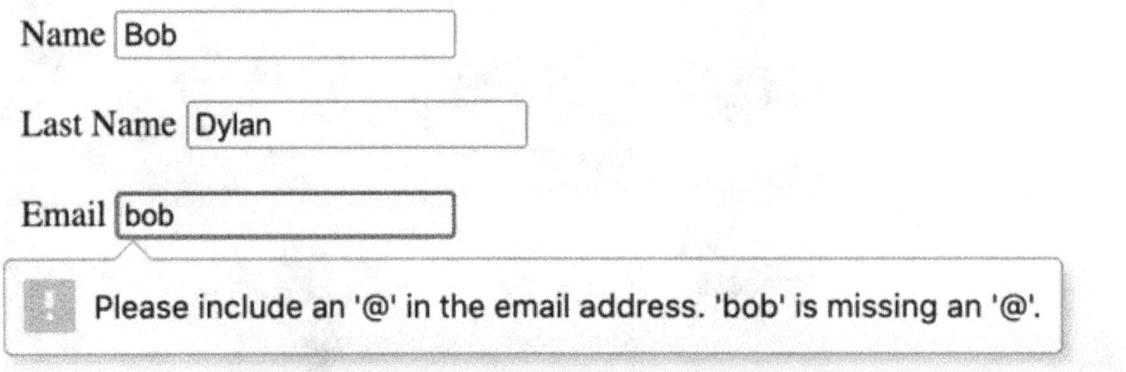

Name Bob

Last Name Dylan

Email bob

! Please include an '@' in the email address. 'bob' is missing an '@'.

Figure 121 - Email type validation

If it is not present it will not be possible to send the data. If you add the at sign, the browser will make sure that there is a text immediately following it (this is the domain of the email address).

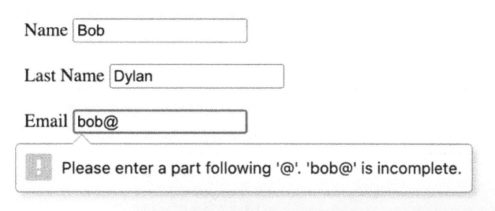

Figure 122 - Email type validation

HTML side validations are not reliable because the code is manipulable on the client side. Real checks are done with other languages and on different levels. However, implementing these HTML side validations is also recommended.

There are never too many checks!

Browsers that do not support this specification will interpret the input with type *text*, so there are no compatibility problems.

An interesting feature of the *email* type is the loading on smartphones and tablets of a customized keypad for entering email addresses. If you acquire the focus on an *<input type = "email">*, from devices other than desktop, the keypad opens with the alphabet in lowercase and the period and at sign characters.

Other types of inputs

file	It allows the user to open their client's filesystem and select a file to upload via the form.
hidden	It is a hidden field that can contain a useful value for the programmer (it cannot be changed by the user).
image	It is a generic button that has the ability to be displayed as an image.
password	It is a field that masks the value entered by the user with dots.
search	It is a similar input to *text*, but exclusively used to create search bars. Always remember to value the name attribute, otherwise the search will not be carried out. The most common *name* value for search inputs is "*q*" (Google's search bar also uses this value).
color	Allows you to select a color using the palette. You can enter a default hexadecimal value with the *value* attribute (eg: #000000 corresponds to black).
number	It allows the insertion of numerical values only. Smartphones and tablets show the numeric keypad when the focus is acquired. The **min** and **max** attributes can be used to limit the

	numeric range that can be entered. For example, *min="20"* and *max="40"* allow the user to enter only values from 20 to 40.
tel	It is the input dedicated to entering the telephone number. Unlike the email and url type, it does not allow dedicated client-side validation because the telephone numbers change from country to country and it is almost impossible to find a common pattern. Although tel-type inputs are identical to text-type inputs, they have different and useful features. The most obvious is that browsers opened from mobile or tablet can choose to display a keypad optimized for entering phone numbers. Furthermore, using a specific input type for telephone numbers makes the development of a custom validation and, more generally, their management easier.
url	It is used to enter web addresses. Smartphones and tablets will show the keypad that contains the period and the main extensions (.com, .it, etc ...).

range	It is a slider through which it is possible to choose a numerical value. The only difference with the type *number* is the graphic rendering, although it is preferable to use it only when the value can be approximate (for example to evaluate the satisfaction of a customer).
date	Allows you to choose a date via a calendar.
month	Similar to dates, but limits the entry to the month and year.
week	Allows you to select the number corresponding to the week within the year.
time	Allows you to select a time.
datetime	Allows you to select date and time.
datetime-local	Allows you to select date and time. The use, compared to the previous *datetime*, is indicated for applications that make use of international times.

Textarea

The *<textarea>* tag allows the user to enter a longer text than what is usually written in the *text* input. It is often used for inserting comments or reviews. It is a multiline input with no limit of characters that can be entered.

```
<label for="textareaHtml">How do you like HTML?</label>
<br>
<textarea id="textareaHtml" name="html"></textarea>
<br>
```

Figure 123 – Textarea (editor)

Also pay attention to the *for* and *id* attributes here in order to associate the *label* to the *textarea* and always remember the *name* attribute on the form fields. It is thanks to the *name* that you will be able to send the data correctly to the back-end to process it.

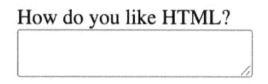

Figure 124 – Textarea (browser)

The *rows* (rows) and *cols* (columns) attributes allow you to specify the exact size to be assumed by the *<textarea>*. Think of them like the rows and columns of an excel sheet. Increasing the numerical value of *rows* will result in a higher textarea, while increasing the *cols* will make it wider. Setting these attributes is always recommended to keep the size of the textarea consistent on all browsers; the default settings of the browsers, in fact, can be different.

If you want to insert default text you must write it as the content between the opening tag and the closing tag because the value attribute is not supported.

```
<label for="textareaHtml">How do you like HTML?</label>
<br>
<textarea id="textareaHtml" name="html" rows="9" cols="35">Placeholder textarea...</textarea>
<br>
```

Figure 125 - Rows and cols attributes and placeholder

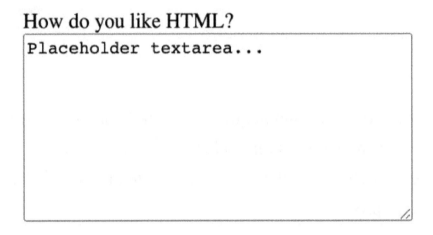

Figure 126 - Rows and cols attributes and placeholder (browser)

Select

The **<select>** element is used to create a drop-down list, also called a picklist or selection menu, useful for making the user select an option. The **<option>** tags within the <select> tag identify, as the name suggests, the options available in the list.

As usual, the *name* attribute is necessary to correctly send the data while the id attribute is necessary to associate the list with a label.

Each <option> tag must have a *value* attribute containing the value of the selected option. If omitted, the default value will be the text contained within the tag. You can also use the *selected* attribute to make an option selected by default on page load.

```
<label for="bandSelect">Pick a band:</label>
<br>
<select name="band" id="bandSelect">
    <option value="pinkfloyd">Pink Floyd</option>
    <option value="muse">Muse</option>
    <option value="greenday" selected>Green Day</option>
    <option value="radiohead">Radiohead</option>
</select>
```

Figure 127 – Select and option tag

Let's reload the page.

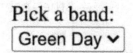

Figure 128 - Select and option tag (browser)

The *"Green Day"* option is selected by default because I have inserted the selected attribute in the relevant *<option tag>*.

Then there are some unique attributes of the select tag:

- **multiple** allows you to view more options by enlarging the selection menu and adding, if necessary, a scrollbar;
- **size** is used to specify how many options should be displayed (see Figure 129).

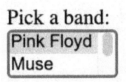

Figure 129 - Multiple attribute and size = "2"

You can also nest multiple *<option>* tags inside *<optgroup>* elements to create separate groups of options within the list.

Additional attributes

maxlength	Allows you to enter a numeric value that limits the insertion of characters. Example: *maxlength="20"* blocks the insertion of the 21st character in the field.
disabled	Disable the field not allowing the

	user to acquire the focus.
autofocus	The user acquires the focus on this field automatically when the page is loaded.

*

In conclusion, I want to remind you that, being the forms composed of HTML tags, they can be worked with CSS for a better graphic rendering.

Figure 130 - CSS allows you to "style" your HTML code

You have the proof of the power of CSS in Figure 130. On the left you have the HTML skeleton of a contact form, on the right you have the same HTML code integrated with style sheets. What's more interesting is that the same HTML skeleton can be graphically worked in many different (potentially infinite) ways. This means that the form you see on the right is only a potential version of what it might look like.

If you believe that you may be interested in studying CSS to integrate the knowledge of HTML you are acquiring, I would like to suggest my guide on CSS, which can be easily found online.

Chapter 7. Other TAGs

Below is the complete list of HTML tags with an invitation to deepen them and experiment with their use. It is clear that a good formatter is not required to know all the tags by heart, but that he has the mindset to propose the right solution for the right case.

Quoting Harry Potter: "Use it well!"

Tag	Description
<!-- commented content -->	Allows you to comment on a portion of text/code. The content of a comment will not be displayed in the browser.
<!DOCTYPE>	Tells the browser what type of document it is opening.
<a>	Link.
<abbr>	Abbreviation or acronym.
<acronym>	Not supported in HTML5. <abbr> is used instead.
<address>	Used for contact information.
<applet>	Not supported in HTML5. You can use <embed> or <object>.
<area>	Area within an "image map" (an image map is an image with clickable areas). See <map> tag.

<article>	Semantic tag for articles.
<aside>	Semantic tag for side content.
<audio>	Embed audio content.
<b>	Bold.
<base>	Indicates the referring URL base for all relative document paths (paths).
<basefont>	Not supported in HTML5. Make graphic changes regarding color, size and font. It uses CSS instead.
<bdi>	It stands for *"Bi-Directional Isolation"* and deals with isolating a portion of text that needs to be formatted in a different direction than the rest (eg a portion of Arabic text in a paragraph in English: *<p> The competitor <bdi>* انا ن *</bdi> scored 10 points </p>*).
<bdo>	Overrides the direction of the text.
<big>	Not supported in HTML5. Makes the text larger. It uses CSS instead.
<blockquote>	Quote.
<body>	Body of the HTML document.
* *	Return by inserting a line break.
<button>	Clickable Button.
<canvas>	It is a container of graphics that can be drawn using programming languages such as Javascript.

<caption>	Title of a table.
<center>	Not supported in HTML5. Centrally aligns a text. It uses CSS instead.
<cite>	Identify the title of an artistic work (song, poem, book, film, etc ...).
<code>	Useful when you want to print code written with markup and programming languages.
<col>	Identifies the columns within *<colgroup>*.
<colgroup>	Group of columns in a table.
<data>	Useful when you want to associate a machine-readable value with a product.
<datalist>	Finds a list of pre-defined options for a form input.
<dd>	Used in conjunction with *<dl>* e *<dt>*. It is used to describe an element of a *<dl>* list.
<del>	Strikethrough.
<details>	Defines an area in which to add additional information that a user can decide to see or not.
<dfn>	It stands for *"definition element"* and identifies a term that will be explained within the document.
<dialog>	Defines a dialog box (a popup)

	within a page.
<dir>	Not supported in HTML5. *<ul>* is used instead.
<div>	Container/section of a document.
<dl>	Description list. It contains *<dt>* and *<dd>*.
<dt>	Used in conjunction with *<dl>* and *<dd>*. Find the name of an item in a description list.
<em>	Italic.
<embed>	Container for an external application.
<fieldset>	Groups a set of inputs to a form.
<figcaption>	*<figure>* tag caption.
<figure>	It defines content such as image, illustration, diagram etc....
<font>	Not supported in HTML5. Defines the type of font, color and size. It uses CSS instead.
<footer>	Semantic tag for the final content of a page.
<form>	Form.
<frame>	Not supported in HTML5. It finds a window in a *<frameset>*.
<frameset>	Contains a *<frameset>*.
Da <h1> a <h6>	Titles/headings.
<head>	Contains information and metadata

	of the document.
<header>	Semantic tag for introductions or navigation link sets.
<hr>	Space line.
<html>	Tag root of a HTML document.
<i>	Italic.
<iframe>	Inline Frame (see chapter 8).
<img>	Image.
<input>	A form input.
<ins>	Indicates a piece of text added later.
<kbd>	Useful for entering keyboard keys when typing a shortcut (ex. Click *<kbd>*Ctrl*</kbd>* + *<kbd>*C*</kbd>* to copy).
<label>	Label for form inputs.
<legend>	*<fieldset>* tag title.
<li>	Single element of a *<ol>* or *<ul>* list.
<link>	Link to an external resource (often a style sheet).
<main>	Semantic tag that identifies the main content of a page.
<map>	Find a "map image". It is an image with clickable areas. Contains one or more *<area>* tags.
<mark>	Highlight the text in yellow.

`<meta>`	Metadata of a document.
`<meter>`	Create a visual measurement given a value within a defined range.
`<nav>`	Semantic tag for navigation menu.
`<noframes>`	Not supported in HTML5. Find alternative content for users who don't support frames.
`<noscript>`	Find alternate content for users who don't support client-side scripts (e.g. javascript).
`<object>`	Container for external resources. It is preferable to use `<img>`, `<iframe>`, `<audio>` and `<video>` when possible.
`<ol>`	Ordered list.
`<optgroup>`	Find a group of options in a drop-down list (`<select>` tag).
`<option>`	`<select>` tag option.
`<output>`	Used to display the result of a calculation.
`<p>`	Paragraph.
`<param>`	Defines a parameter for the `<object>` tag.
`<picture>`	Container for images of different types.
`<pre>`	Preformatted text. The browser does not interpret the content, but only

	prints it.
<progress>	Progress bar.
<q>	Short quote.
<rp>	Tells the browser what to show in case *ruby markup* is not supported.
<rt>	Indicates an explanation or pronunciation of the characters (for East Asian typography) in a *ruby* annotation. It is contained in *<ruby>*.
<ruby>	A *ruby* annotation is a small extra text, attached to the main text, to indicate the pronunciation or meaning of the corresponding characters. It is often used in Japanese publications. It is used with *<rt>* and *<rp>*.
<s>	Strikethrough.
<samp>	Used to print computer output messages in the browser. The difference with *<code>* is only semantics.
<script>	Used to write client-side scripts (eg Javascript).
<section>	Semantic tag for generic sections.
<select>	Drop-down list (selection list).

<source>	Used within *<audio>*, *<video>* and *<picture>* to locate the multimedia resource we want to show.
<span>	It is an inline tag with no effects. It is useful when you need to embed content within a tag without inheriting particular formatting.
<strike>	Not supported in HTML5. Strikethrough effect.
<strong>	Bold used to identify keywords.
<style>	Used to embed CSS within an HTML file.
<sub>	Subscript.
<summary>	Visible and clickable title to show the contents of *<details>*.
<sup>	Apex.
<svg>	Container for svg.
<table>	Table.
<tbody>	Contains the body of a table.
<td>	Cell of a table.
<template>	Container for content hidden on page load. It is displayed later with Javascript if necessary.
<textarea>	Multiline input.
<tfoot>	Footer of a table.
<th>	Cell containing the title of a column

	in a table.
\<thead\>	Contains the titles of the individual columns.
\<time\>	Used to contain a time, date or occurrence.
\<tr\>	Row of a table.
\<track\>	Used for subtitles, captions or other files containing text to be displayed when a media (*\<audio\>* or *\<video\>*) is playing.
\<tt\>	Not supported in HTML5. It is a "monospaced" text tag (all letters occupy the same space). It uses CSS instead.
\<ul\>	Unordered list.
\<u\>	Underlined.
\<var\>	Find a variable in math or programming expressions.
\<video\>	Embed of video contents.
\<wbr\>	Used to add potential line-break. It is used to avoid the possibility of browsers wrapping a very long word in a wrong place.

Chapter 8. Final project

With this final project we try to summarize the knowledge acquired so far. We will create three linked pages: a homepage with an article on Beethoven, a contact page and a page with the classical compositions of the artists we will mention.

Let's begin!

Homepage

Let's create our first file and name it "*index.html*". The name *index* is usually used for the main page of a website (homepage). This is because when you reach a website without specifying the html resource to open (for example: "*www.mywebsite.com*" and not "*www.mywebsite.com/about-us.html*"), it points to an entire folder (ie our root). In this case the webserver looks for a resource named *index.html* by default (or also *index.php*, it depends on the languages used) and it opens it. If the programmer does not insert this resource and, consequently, the webserver does not find it, you can run into unpleasant errors such as viewing the entire directory of your site (list of all the files contained in your root).
Always remember to rename your main page *index.html*.

Before doing that, let's create a folder named *root*. Inside we create *index.html* and write the basic structure. In the *<title>* inside *<head>* we write *Home*. Before working on *index.html* let's structure our root. We create an *images* folder where we will insert the images we will need and a *Documents* folder where we will insert the other two HTML pages.

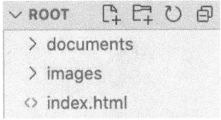

Figure 145 – Root structure

We structure our index with the semantic tags, seen in Chapter 6. We will need a *<header>* for the logo, a *<main>* for the main section and a

<footer>.

```
<> index.html  ×

...
 1   <!DOCTYPE html>
 2   <html>
 3
 4       <head>
 5           <meta charset="utf-8">
 6           <title>Home</title>
 7       </head>
 8
 9       <body>
10
11           <header></header>
12
13           <main></main>
14
15           <footer></footer>
16
17       </body>
18
19   </html>
20
```

Figure 146 - Index.html

We add a logo to the *<header>*. You can use any logo you have available. The ideal would be a .png or a .svg. I will use for this example the logo of an old music startup of mine named *musicfinder*. Here is the link of the image with which you can download it and use it for this exercise: https://www.musicfinder.it/wp-content/uploads/2018/01/logoBiancoCompleto-1024x866.png. Save it in the *images* folder renaming it *logo.png*.

```
<header>
    <img src="images/logo.png" width="70">
</header>
```

Figure 147 - Logo in <header>

You will have immediately noticed that the logo is white as the background color. In this way the image is not visible in the browser.

We have two possible solutions:

1. export a new version of the logo of another color (eg black);
2. specify a new background color for the entire page or for the single *<header>* with CSS.

Instead of giving you the logo of another color, I prefer to apply some CSS in order to anticipate something of this new mark-up language. If you want to learn more about style sheets and you liked this guide on HTML, I would like to recommend you again the purchase of my second volume entirely dedicated to CSS. It can be considered as the continuation of this guide.

To apply a background color to the *<header>* tag write as follows:

```
<header style="background: #ff9216">
        <img src="images/logo.png" width="70">
</header>
```

Basically we are telling the browser that everything contained within the *style* attribute must be read and interpreted as CSS and not as HTML. I add some *padding* to distance the logo from the edges of the *<header>* tag. Think of padding as the *cellpadding* of a cell; it is in fact the space between the edge of the tag and its content. To add another CSS instruction just divide it from the previous one with a ";".

```
<header style="background:  #ff9216; padding: 10px;">
    <img src="images/logo.png" width="70">
</header>
```

Figure 148 - Background color and padding in CSS3

Let's see what happens in the browser.

Figure 149 - Background color and padding

As you can see, the background color of the *<header>* tag has changed and space has been added to its borders and the image it contains. If we hadn't written the *padding* instruction, the logo would have been attached to the edges.

Let's proceed with the formatting of the page. As a text I will use extracts from the Wikipedia page dedicated to Beethoven. Let's start by inserting, within *<main>*, a title *<h1>* with the name of the German composer, separating it with a <hr> from the italicized writing "*By Wikipedia, the free encyclopedia.*".

```
<main>
    <h1>Ludwig van Beethoven</h1>

    <hr>

    <em>By Wikipedia, the free encyclopedia</em>
</main>
```

Figure 150 - <h1>, <hr> and <em>

We then insert three paragraphs.

```
<p>
    <b>Ludwig van Beethoven</b> (baptised 17 December 1770 – 26 March 1827) was a German composer and
    pianist.
</p>

<p>
    Beethoven remains one of the most admired composers in the history of Western music; his works rank
    amongst the most performed of the <a href="https://en.wikipedia.org/wiki/Classical_music"
    target="_blank" title="Classical music">classical music</a> repertoire, and span the transition from
    the classical period to the romantic era in classical music.
</p>

<p>
    His career has conventionally been divided into early, middle, and late periods. <br>The "early"
    period, during which he forged his craft, is typically considered to have lasted until 1802. From 1802
    to around 1812, his "middle" period showed an individual development from the "classical" styles of <a
    href="https://en.wikipedia.org/wiki/Joseph_Haydn" target="_blank" title="Joseph Haydn">Joseph Haydn</
    a> and <a href="https://en.wikipedia.org/wiki/Wolfgang_Amadeus_Mozart" target="_blank" title="Wolfgang
    Amadeus Mozart">Wolfgang Amadeus Mozart</a>, and is sometimes characterized as "heroic". <b>During
    this time, he began to suffer increasingly from deafness</b>. In his "late" period from 1812 to his
    death in 1827, he extended his innovations in musical form and expression.
</p>
```

Figure 151 - <p>, <a>, <br> and <b>

Inside them I added a couple of *<b>* tags for the bold, three links pointing to the wikipedia pages *Classical Music*, *Haydn* and *Mozart* (note the title tags to make the tooltip appear if you move the cursor over the element) and *
*. Now reload the file in your browser. You should see something like this:

Ludwig van Beethoven

By Wikipedia, the free encyclopedia

Ludwig van Beethoven (baptised 17 December 1770 – 26 March 1827) was a German composer and pianist.

Beethoven remains one of the most admired composers in the history of Western music; his works rank amongst the most performed of the classical music repertoire, and span the transition from the classical period to the romantic era in classical music.

His career has conventionally been divided into early, middle, and late periods. The "early" period, during which he forged his craft, is typically considered to have lasted until 1802. From 1802 to around 1812, his "middle" period showed an individual development from the "classical" styles of Joseph Haydn and Wolfgang Amadeus Mozart, and is sometimes characterized as "heroic". **During this time, he began to suffer increasingly from deafness.** In his "late" period from 1812 to his death in 1827, he extended his innovations in musical form and expression.

Figure 152 - Beethoven article

We now insert an unordered list with the most important Beethoven influences. Immediately after, we insert a link to our internal page with the compositions of the musicians mentioned in the list. Let's name the file *"compositions.html"* and insert it in the *documents* folder.

```
<section>
    <h4>Influences of Ludwig van Beethoven:</h3>
    <ul>
        <li>Wolfgang Amadeus Mozart</li>
        <li>Johann Sebastian Bach</li>
        <li>Franz Joseph Haydn</li>
        <li>Georg Friedrich Händel</li>
    </ul>
    <a href="documents/compositions.html">
        <b>Listen to the compositions of each of these classic artists here</b>
    </a>
</section>
```

Figure 153 - Section influences with <ul>

I used a title *<h4>*, bold for the content of the link *<a>* and I put everything inside another semantic tag *<section>*.

This produces something like the following in a browser.

Influences of Ludwig van Beethoven:

- Wolfgang Amadeus Mozart
- Johann Sebastian Bach
- Franz Joseph Haydn
- Georg Friedrich Händel

Listen to the compositions of each of these classic artists here

Figure 154 - Influences section in the browser

I want to change the link color using a new CSS statement. Write as in Figure 155 and you will see that the color will change from blue to pink.

```
<a href="documents/compositions.html" style="color: ■#FF0066">
    <b>Listen to the compositions of each of these classic artists here</b>
</a>
```

Figure 155 - CSS "color" statement

Let's reload the page.

Influences of Ludwig van Beethoven:

- Wolfgang Amadeus Mozart
- Johann Sebastian Bach
- Franz Joseph Haydn
- Georg Friedrich Händel

Listen to the compositions of each of these classic artists here

Figure 156 - Link color changed

Before working on the page dedicated to compositions, we conclude the homepage with a footer showing the name of the author of the article and a link to the third internal page dedicated to contacts. Let's take space from the main with two *
* tags and a *<hr>* tag and open the *<footer>* tag.

```
    </main>

    <br>
    <hr>
    <br>

    <footer></footer>
```

Figure 157 – Space between <main> and <footer>

Inside we simply write the author name and link in italics. To better graphically detach the footer from the rest of the page, I would apply, as done for the header, a cream background color and a slight padding.

```
<footer style="background:☐#fff7e5; padding:10px;">
    <p>
        <em>Author: John Doe – <a href="documents/contacts.html">Contacts</a></em>
    </p>
</footer>
```

Figure 158 - Background color and padding

Let's reload the page.

Author: John Doe · Contacts

Figure 159 – Footer (browser)

Here's what our homepage looks like at this point.

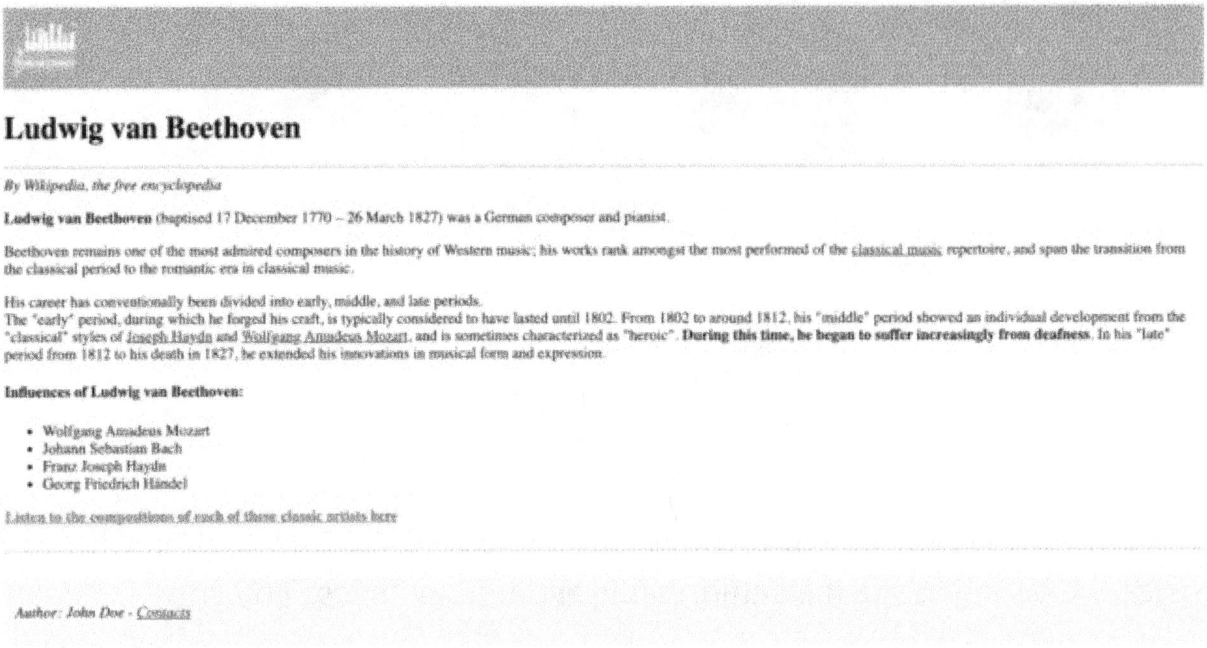

Ludwig van Beethoven

By Wikipedia, the free encyclopedia

Ludwig van Beethoven (baptised 17 December 1770 – 26 March 1827) was a German composer and pianist.

Beethoven remains one of the most admired composers in the history of Western music; his works rank amongst the most performed of the classical music repertoire, and span the transition from the classical period to the romantic era in classical music.

His career has conventionally been divided into early, middle, and late periods.
The "early" period, during which he forged his craft, is typically considered to have lasted until 1802. From 1802 to around 1812, his "middle" period showed an individual development from the "classical" styles of Joseph Haydn and Wolfgang Amadeus Mozart, and is sometimes characterized as "heroic". **During this time, he began to suffer increasingly from deafness.** In his "late" period from 1812 to his death in 1827, he extended his innovations in musical form and expression.

Influences of Ludwig van Beethoven:

- Wolfgang Amadeus Mozart
- Johann Sebastian Bach
- Franz Joseph Haydn
- Georg Friedrich Händel

Listen to the compositions of each of these classic artists here

Author: John Doe - Contacts

Figure 160 – Homepage

Finally, let's change the page font. As we mentioned during the guide, the default font is Times New Roman. To change it we need another CSS instruction that we will give directly to the *<body>* tag. In this way, all the tags contained within *<body>* will inherit the instruction that changes the font, so the page will have a uniform one. **Cascading inheritance** is the first and fundamental characteristic of CSS (it is no coincidence that CSS stands for Cascading Style Sheets). As I said before, I make these small changes with CSS to give you a very small hint of its potential and to entice you to study it further. I don't dwell on the detailed explanation because it is not the subject of this guide.

To change the font from Times New Roman to Helvetica write as follows (I take this opportunity to also apply a gray text color instead of black).

```
<body style="font-family: Helvetica, sans-serif; color: rgb(78, 78, 78)">
```

Figure 161 - Font-family and color statement

Reload the page and make sure that the result is as in the following Figure.

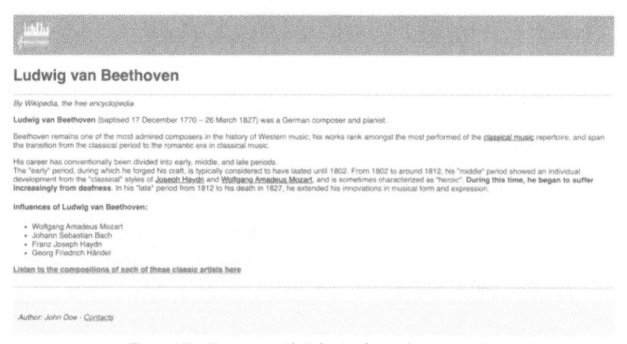

Figure 162 - Homepage with Helvetica font and gray text color

If you notice any errors or differences with your homepage, follow carefully all the steps I have performed again and carefully check the opening and closing of the tags.

Music page

Open the previously created *compositions.html* file and write the basic structure of the document by inserting *"Compositions"* in the *<title>* tag. Copy and paste the *<header>* tag, with its content, from *index.html* so that you have the same header in this file as well (**attention**: the relative path of the logo changes because *compositions.html* is located inside the *documents* folder). To keep the pages uniform between them, I also apply the Helvetica font and the dark gray color here.

```
<!DOCTYPE html>
<html>

    <head>
        <meta charset="utf-8">
        <title>Compositions</title>
    </head>

    <body style="font-family: Helvetica, sans-serif; color: rgb(78, 78, 78)">

        <header style="background: #ff9216; padding:10px;">
            <img src="../images/logo.png" width="70">
        </header>

    </body>

</html>
```
Figure 163 - Header in compositions.html page

Save three *.jpeg* files depicting Mozart, Bach and Haydn in the *images* folder and insert them under the header inside the *<main>* tag. We also write a title *<h1>*, a link to return to the homepage and a title *<h3>* to introduce the images. We add a fixed width and height to the images in order to make them equal to each other and also insert the *alt* attribute to specify an alternative text if the image is not loaded.

```
<main>

    <h1>Compositions</h1>

    <a href="../index.html">Go back to homepage</a>

    <h3>Images with link</h3>

    <img src="../images/mozart.jpeg" alt="Wolfgang Amadeus Mozart image" width="200" height="250">

    <img src="../images/haydn.jpeg" alt="Franz Joseph Haydn image" width="200" height="250">

    <img src="../images/bach.jpeg" alt="Johann Sebastian Bach image" width="200" height="250">

</main>
```
Figure 164 - <main> tag with images

Let's reload the page.

Figure 165 - compositions.html page in the browser

At this point we can incorporate the images within the <*a*> tag to redirect, upon clicking on them, users to the YouTube video of the chosen composition. I will use the "Best Of" of these three artists.

```
<h1>Compositions</h1>

<a href="../index.html">Go back to homepage</a>

<h3>Images with link</h3>

<a href="https://www.youtube.com/watch?v=Rb0UmrCXxVA" target="_blank" title="The Best of Mozart: listen on
YouTube">
    <img src="../images/mozart.jpeg" alt="Wolfgang Amadeus Mozart image" width="200" height="250">
</a>

<a href="https://www.youtube.com/watch?v=EmZF3kBZO6E" target="_blank" title="The Best of Haydn: listen on
YouTube">
    <img src="../images/haydn.jpeg" alt="Franz Joseph Haydn image" width="200" height="250">
</a>

<a href="https://www.youtube.com/watch?v=6JQm5aSjX6g" target="_blank" title="The Best of Bach: listen on
YouTube">
    <img src="../images/bach.jpeg" alt="Johann Sebastian Bach image" width="200" height="250">
</a>
```

Figure 166 - <a> tag for clickable images

Now when you click on the images, the chosen video will open in a new tab.

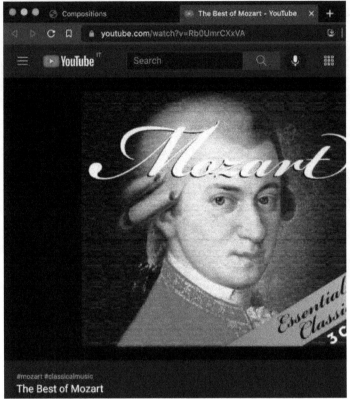

Figure 167 - Redirect on YouTube

We draw a dividing line with *<hr>* and embed three other videos using iFrame as done in chapter 8. We then choose the video to embed, click on "Share", select "Embed" and copy the HTML code that is automatically generated by YouTube.

```
<h3>iFrame</h3>

<iframe width="280" height="157" src="https://www.youtube.com/embed/W-fFHeTX78Q" title="YouTube video
player" frameborder="0" allow="accelerometer; autoplay; clipboard-write; encrypted-media; gyroscope;
picture-in-picture" allowfullscreen></iframe>

<iframe width="280" height="157" src="https://www.youtube.com/embed/joVkx28oVIg" title="YouTube video
player" frameborder="0" allow="accelerometer; autoplay; clipboard-write; encrypted-media; gyroscope;
picture-in-picture" allowfullscreen></iframe>

<iframe width="280" height="157" src="https://www.youtube.com/embed/Q6NRLYUTkrY" title="YouTube video
player" frameborder="0" allow="accelerometer; autoplay; clipboard-write; encrypted-media; gyroscope;
picture-in-picture" allowfullscreen></iframe>
```

Figure 168 - Embed through iFrame

I have scaled the width and height by 50% from 560 to 280 and 315 to 157 respectively. Our above code would give us the following result.

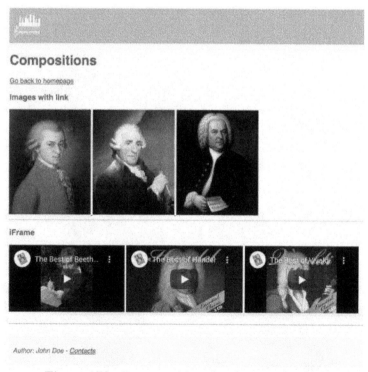

Figure 169 – iFrame (browser)

We copy and paste the footer <u>(remember to change the relative path of the link to the contact page)</u> that we have worked on in the index and reload the page.

Figure 170 - " compositions.html" page finished

What you see in Figure 170 is the final result.

Contact page

On the third and last page we go to insert a contact form including the fields:

- First name;
- Surname;
- Email;
- Favorite composer;
- Textarea;
- *File* type input to attach your favorite composition.

Here too we use the *<header>* tag of the other two files and write the page name inside the *<h1>* tag contained in the *<main>*.

Let's proceed with the construction of the form by opening the *<form>* tag and enhancing the three main attributes *name, action* and *method*.

```html
<!DOCTYPE html>
<html>

    <head>
        <meta charset="utf-8">
        <title>Contacts</title>
    </head>

    <body style="font-family: Helvetica, sans-serif; color:▉rgb(78, 78, 78)">

        <header style="background:▉#ff9216; padding:10px;">
            <img src="../images/logo.png" width="70">
        </header>

        <main>

            <h1>Contacts</h1>

            <form name="contactForm" action="server.php" method="get">

            </form>

        </main>
```

Figure 171 - Tag <form>

Let's write the first three inputs dedicated to entering the name, surname and email address. Let's make them mandatory with the *required* attribute. Never forget the *name* attribute; if omitted it will not be possible to associate the value sent to the back-end. We use the *<label>* tags as seen in the chapter dedicated to Forms.

```html
<label>Name*
    <br>
    <input type="text" name="name" placeholder="e.g. John" required>
</label>
<br>
<br>
<label>Last Name*
    <br>
    <input type="text" name="lastname" placeholder="e.g. Doe" required>
</label>
<br>
<br>
<label>Email*
    <br>
    <input type="email" name="email" placeholder="e.g. john@doe.com" required>
</label>
```

Figure 172 - Input for name, surname and email

Then we insert a group of radio inputs to let the user select the preferred composer. Also in this case we act as seen in chapter 9.

```
<br>
<br>
<br>
Who is your favorite classical composer?
<br>
<br>
<input type="radio" id="composer1" name="composer" value="Mozart">
<label for="composer1">Mozart</label>
<br>
<input type="radio" id="composer2" name="composer" value="Vivaldi">
<label for="composer2">Vivaldi</label>
<br>
<input type="radio" id="composer3" name="composer" value="Bach">
<label for="composer3">Bach</label>
<br>
<input type="radio" id="composer4" name="composer" value="Beethoven">
<label for="composer4">Beethoven</label>
<br>
<br>
<br>
```

Figure 173 - Radio input group

Let's reload the page to see the progress up to this point.

Contacts

Name*

e.g. John

Last Name*

e.g. Doe

Email*

e.g. john@doe.com

Who is your favorite classical composer?

○ Mozart
○ Vivaldi
○ Bach
○ Beethoven

Figure 174 – Form (browser)

We now insert a textarea to allow the user to motivate his choice and allow, through a *file* type input, to attach the audio file of his favorite composition.

```
<br>
<label for="textareaHtml">Why?</label>
<br>
<textarea id="textareaHtml" name="html" rows="9" cols="35"></textarea>
<br>
<br>
<br>
<label for="composition">Attach the mp3 file of your favorite composition:</label>
<br>
<input type="file" id="composition" name="composition" accept=".mp3">
<br>
<br>
<br>
<input type="submit" value="Submit">
<input type="reset" value="Reset">
</form>
```

Figure 175 - Textarea and file type input

The optional *accept* attribute allows you to specify the type of file that can be attached. In this case, only files with the *.mp3* extension will be accepted. Finally, we insert the two buttons to send the data or clear the fields and close the *<form>* tag.

We reload the page and fill out the form.

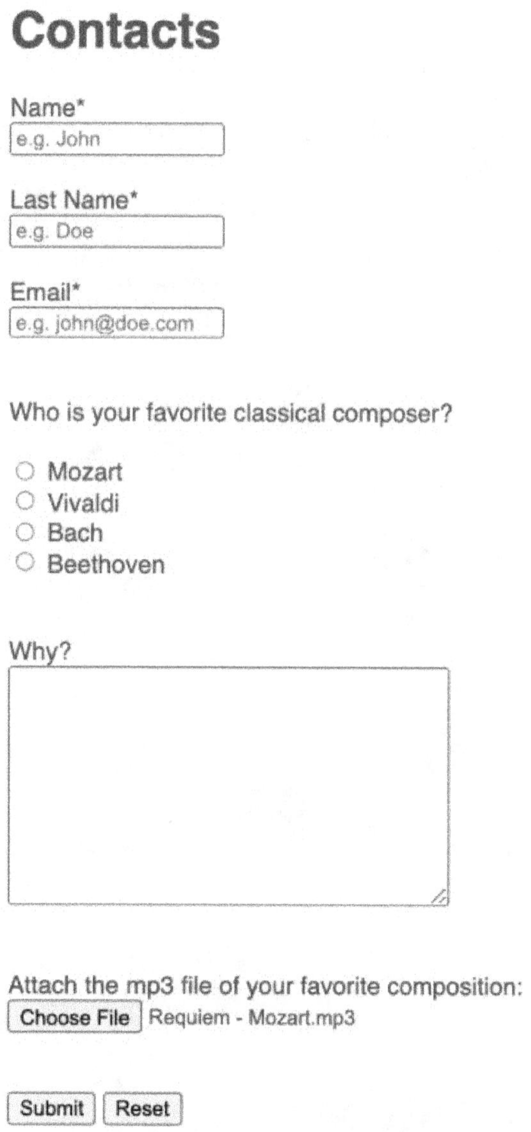

Contacts

Name*

e.g. John

Last Name*

e.g. Doe

Email*

e.g. john@doe.com

Who is your favorite classical composer?

○ Mozart
○ Vivaldi
○ Bach
○ Beethoven

Why?

Attach the mp3 file of your favorite composition:

Choose File   Requiem - Mozart.mp3

Submit   Reset

Figure 176 – Filled form (browser)

Finally, we also close the *<main>* tag, take space with two *
* and a *<hr>* and paste the *<footer>* previously used, taking care to replace the link to the contact page (we are already there!) with the link for return to the Homepage.

```
    </main>

    <br>
    <hr>
    <br>

    <footer style="background:□#fff7e5; padding:10px;">
        <p>
            <em>Author: John Doe - <a href="../index.html">Homepage</a></em>
        </p>
    </footer>
</body>
```

Figure 177 – Contacts page footer

Here is the final result:

Contacts

Name*
e.g. John

Last Name*
e.g. Doe

Email*
e.g. john@doe.com

Who is your favorite classical composer?

○ Mozart
○ Vivaldi
○ Bach
○ Beethoven

Why?

Attach the mp3 file of your favorite composition:
Choose File No file chosen

Submit   Reset

Author: John Doe - Homepage

Figure 178 - Contact page completed

Congratulations, you've just finished your first HTML project!

If you notice any differences or errors, don't be disheartened, rather roll up your sleeves and check your code line by line.

The error is somewhere there!

Conclusion

We have come to the conclusion of this HTML5 study path. It should be clear by now why it is important to know this language: it is essential in the formatting and layout of web pages. It is the official language of web design and the figure of the front-end developer. All sites (from Facebook to the small showcase site of your favorite restaurant) share the use of HTML.

The study of this mark-up language brings you closer to the world of programming. Getting your hands dirty with HTML allows you to learn the basic concepts of coding in a simple and intuitive way and can therefore facilitate the study of programming languages (Javascript, Php, C ++ etc ...).

If you are willing to continue your journey into the world of web-oriented formatting and programming, my advice is to continue with the study of CSS. As you have already understood, it is another mark-up language that we can define as "complementary" to HTML. In fact, it allows you to make the most of the HTML code by customizing, to your liking, the graphics and the arrangement of the components of the web pages.

You will see that the world of web-oriented programming will never cease to amaze you. Every time one door closes, ten doors open. As soon as you have learned to handle HTML and CSS carefully, the world of Javascript opens up. From there you will find yourself facing the (increasingly requested) Js frameworks such as Angular, React and Vue. You will bang your nose on jQuery and Typescript and then get passionate about the world of the back-end with php, Java, node.js etc ...

Not to mention the world of databases!

I could go on and on, but I don't think that's the case. In my small way I hope I have piqued your curiosity and I hope that you will make the most of the opportunities that this world offers both in terms of healthy personal growth and in the workplace.